Designing Greeting Cards and Paper Products

The Art & Design Series

For beginners, students, and professionals in both fine and commercial arts, these books offer practical how-to introductions to a variety of areas in contemporary art and design.

Each illustrated volume is written by a working artist, a specialist in his or her field, and each concentrates on an individual area—from advertising layout or printmaking to interior design, painting, and cartooning, among others. Each contains information that artists will find useful in the studio, in the classroom, and in the marketplace.

Among the titles:

Ron Lister

Designing Greeting Cards and Paper Products

A Complete Guide

 A Spectrum Book • Prentice-Hall, Inc., Englewood Cliffs, New Jersey 07632

Library of Congress Cataloging in Publication Data

Lister, Ron.
　　Designing greeting cards and paper products.

　　(The art & design series)
　　"A Spectrum Book."
　　Bibliography: p.
　　Includes index.
　　1. Greeting cards.　2. Paper products.　3. Commercial
art.　I. Title.　II. Series.
NC1860.L57　1984　　　　741.68′4　　　83-23017
ISBN 0-13-201880-2
ISBN 0-13-201872-1 (pbk.)

This book is available at a special discount when ordered
in bulk quantities. Contact Prentice-Hall, Inc.,
General Publishing Division, Special Sales,
Englewood Cliffs, N.J. 07632.

10　9　8　7　6　5　4　3　2　1

A Spectrum Book. Printed in the United States of America

Title page photos (counterclockwise from upper left)
are as follows:
Figure 0-1 *Zebras,* © Barbara Berger. Courtesy of the artist.
Figure 0-2 By Marshall Joyce. Courtesy of Red Farm Studio.
Figure 0-3 A calendar card for 1884 by Louis Prang.

Production/editorial supervision by Chris McMorrow
Book design by Alice R. Mauro
Cover design by Hal Siegel
Manufacturing buyers: Edward J. Ellis and Doreen Cavallo

Prentice-Hall International, Inc., *London*
Prentice-Hall of Australia Pty. Limited, *Sydney*
Prentice-Hall Canada Inc., *Toronto*
Prentice-Hall of India Private Limited, *New Delhi*
Prentice-Hall of Japan, Inc., *Tokyo*
Prentice-Hall of Southeast Asia Pte. Ltd., *Singapore*
Whitehall Books Limited, *Wellington, New Zealand*
Editora Prentice-Hall do Brasil Ltda., *Rio de Janeiro*

ISBN 0-13-201880-2

ISBN 0-13-201872-1 {PBK.}

This book is dedicated to Jan for her patience and support.

*Working on this project has been a real pleasure
thanks to the help and support of my friends
at Rustcraft and Red Farm Studio,
and to those newly acquired friends
made through contact on this book.*

*I would also like to express my appreciation
to all the various card publishers
whose works are presented in this book.*

Contents

Preface

Figure 0-4
"You're Missed," © Wallace Tripp.
Courtesy of Pawprints, Inc., Jaffry, New Hampshire.

The greeting card field is large and diverse. Viewed singularly, cards are small and relatively simple in design; but when viewed as a collective enterprise, cards represent a multibillion-dollar-a-year industry. As individual designers, we may strive to produce one or two cards per week. The larger card companies produce several million cards a day, and it does not end there. Greeting cards are just part of the larger *paper product* field, which encompasses everything from stationery, party goods, and label design to various forms of fabric, tile, and ceramic design. In fact, most graphics begin on paper, whether the end product is made of paper or not. For example, decorative plates, candles, and ornaments, as well as products made of a variety of other materials from plastic to concrete, are first designed on paper.

This book is intended to be a complete guide for those who wish to become or to continue on as card and paper product artists. Whether you are interested in the field as a hobby or wish to

Figure 0-5
By Ron Lister. Used by permission
of Norcross-Rust Craft divisions
of Windsor Communications Group, Inc.

freelance or work full-time, this book will help. It is also intended to guide those who are planning to design, market, and sell their own cards.

The reader is encouraged to cover as much of the text as possible. The chapters discuss separate topics wherever possible, but much of the information is interrelated and cannot be covered in just one context.

Included along with the general text are designs by and interviews with other artists. An industry this diverse cannot be presented solely from the viewpoint of one person. With me and my colleagues, a more complete perspective is achieved.

Finally, in many places throughout this book, the term *card designers* or simply *designers* has been substituted for the longer *card and paper product designers* in order to simplify the text. These two fields are very closely related and will be discussed separately when necessary.

How does one become a card designer? What sort of background is required? These questions can be answered only in general terms, because card designers come from a wide variety of backgrounds. There are no special art programs for greeting cards, and as a result no Master of Fine Cards degrees either.

The card industry is a commercial enterprise, but it has a fine arts orientation at its base. As a result, many designers have totally dissimilar backgrounds. Some have training in commercial art areas: illustration, fashion, advertising, and the like. Others have fine arts degrees in painting or printing; and still others have no formal training at all.

Degrees do not sell art. It is talent that shows and talent that sells.

The card field is also one place where women have the opportunity to compete with men on equal terms. Although exceptions may be found, good card companies are looking for good cards wherever they come from.

My Introduction to Cards

About twelve years ago, I quite suddenly found myself painting greeting cards, and, much to my surprise, I liked it. I had graduated the previous year with an M.F.A. degree and had moved from Ohio to Boston in search of work. I soon discovered that my fine arts background was of little use in the commercial world. I tried teaching high school and barely escaped with my sanity. After applying at various advertising departments and agencies, I had a clear idea of what I did not want to be.

Finally, I applied and was hired at Rust Craft, a large card publisher located just south of Boston. I stayed for five years, during which time I

Figure 0-6
By Anatoly Dverin. Used by permission
of Norcross-Rust Craft Divisions
of Windsor Communications Group, Inc.

became interested in all aspects of the business. My duties at Rust Craft, besides boardwork, included taking tour groups through the various departments, lecturing at local colleges and schools, and occasionally reviewing portfolios submitted to the company. My stay at Rust Craft was in most ways a very pleasant and informative one.

Before leaving, I built up a freelance clientele and then settled into being on my own for the next two years. In the following years, I moved into teaching fine arts and commercial art and writing. I still consider myself a fine arts painter and show my pastels and oils as often as possible. I am currently freelancing part-time and teaching.

Finally, the people I have met along the way have been good people, creative artists with backgrounds as diverse as imaginable. There has never been a clear division in this field between fine art and commercial art; all of us seem to exist somewhere in between.

Who Buys Cards?

The card market is still basically a woman's market. The majority of cards purchased, whether masculine or feminine in style, are bought by women.

In designing as well, women easily outnumber men. During my career, I estimate that four out of every five designers and potential designers I have met were women; and as a man, I can happily say that I have never felt discriminated against.

Figure 0-7
By Ron Lister. Used by permission
of Norcross-Rust Craft Divisions
of Windsor Communications Group, Inc.

Figure 0-8
Judy Mitchell's *Holly Hobbie Dolls*,
© 1983 American Greetings Corp. Courtesy
of GORHAM DIVISION OF TEXTRON, INC.,
Providence, Rhode Island (licensee).

Card Design

Figure 0-9 Ogata Korin, (Japanese, 1658–1716), "Cranes." Courtesy of H. George Caspari, Inc. and the Freer Gallery of Art, Smithsonian Institution, Washington, D.C.

Chapter One

A Short History of Greeting Cards

Figure 1-1 Christmas card, circa 1900. Courtesy Recycled Paper Products, Inc., Chicago, Illinois.

Any history of greeting cards is bound to include a history of celebrated occasions, starting with the oldest and most universal occasion, New Years. The first day of the year has been special to people as long as calendars have recorded the event. As far back as 700 B.C., the Egyptians gave New Years gifts accompanied by messages of well-being. The Chinese, too, have celebrated the new year for centuries through poetry and painting. New Years greetings were also known in Roman times. Copies of medallions have survived that were addressed to the emperor Hadrian (A.D. 117 to 138). They bear a portrait of Hadrian on the front and carry the following message, somewhat abbreviated, on the back: "The Senate and People of Rome wish a Happy and Prosperous New Year to Hadrianus Augustus, the father of the country." [1]

The exchanging of New Years sentiments followed an uneven course throughout the next thousand years, due primarily to the inconsistent nature of Western European society as a whole. Sentiments began to flourish once again, however, in Germany during the fifteenth and sixteenth centuries. The popularity of these prints (woodcuts) began to spread throughout Europe and especially in Austria, where "dainty handmade creations were offered in an almost endless variety . . ." [2] until the nineteenth century.

THE FIRST CARDS IN ENGLAND

Although New Years has remained a popular holiday throughout history, it was the celebration of Christmas that produced the first officially recognized cards. Artist John Calcott Horsley, of England, is credited with sending the first card. The surviving copy, which was originally sent to artist Henry Cole, was signed in the form of a self-caricature and clearly dated by the artist, 1843.

The idea of making personal Christmas cards became very popular, and England had a new pastime. For nineteen years, card-sending remained a personal venture, but in 1862, Charles Goodall and Sons issued the first card series for general use. Within five years, large-scale publishing began with Marcus Ward and Company. In the following years, many noted artists and illustrators worked for Ward. Perhaps the most highly regarded of these was Kate Greenaway, the famous illustrator of children's books, who illustrated such classics as *The Pied Piper of Hamlin* and *Mother Goose.*

The first card inserts were published in 1884 by Hildesheimer and Company.

Christmas Card Mania

Between 1862 and 1890, the sending of both personally made and manufactured Christmas cards flourished with incredible consistency. In

an 1894 edition of the magazine *The Studio*, an article appeared entitled "Christmas Cards and Their Designers," written by Gleason White. In his story, White quoted as his chief source a Mr. Jonathan King, a greeting card collector who was clearly the authority of his day. He wrote that

Figure 1-2
Louis Prang Christmas floral, circa 1880. Prang is credited with being the "father" of American greeting cards. He worked in Boston from 1856 until 1890.

---

[1] Ernest Dudley Chase, *The Romance of Greeting Cards* (Cambridge: University Press of Cambridge, Rust Craft Publishers, 1956), pp. 10–11. Used by permission.

[2] Chase, *Greeting Cards*, p. 12.

the King collection, ". . . included over seven hundred volumes of cards, weighing between six and seven tons and included approximately 163,000 varieties of cards . . ."—an amazing number of cards for one person to collect. [3]

The cards that appeared in England during the 1870s and 1880s were generally of the finest quality and sophistication of their day. These cards were sold primarily on the artist's design alone. No written sentiment except for a simple "Merry Christmas" or "Happy New Year" normally accompanied the artwork. As written sentiments did become fashionable, quotes from the Old Testament were used as well as from notable authors of the day such as Charles Dickens.

During the 1890s a general decline in card-sending and sales took place, and many quality companies folded as a result.

AMERICAN CARDS

The early course of American cards followed a path similar to England's. Cards flourished in increasing numbers throughout the 1870s and 1880s, only to experience a drastic decline in the 1890s. For roughly a dozen years, the American industry suffered as did the English market, but near the end of the first decade of the twentieth century most of the major publishers we know of today were being founded in Kansas City, Philadelphia, and Boston. In a general sense, the American card industry can be divided into two periods: those years before 1890 and those years after 1909–1910.

Those first twenty years clearly belong to one man, Louis Prang, an exile from the German revolution of 1848. Prang founded a small lithographic printing business in Roxbury, a section of Boston, in 1856. Obsessed with quality in all his endeavors, Prang had perfected his own multicolor printing process by 1866. He called his prints *chromos*. Never satisfied, he continually refined and improved on his printing. Eventually, even fine oil paintings could be reproduced to such perfection that experts could not tell the original from the print without close scrutiny.

Prang printed his first Christmas cards in 1874 and shipped them to England, where an established market awaited. Soon his designs became popular in the U.S. as well, and with good reason. Although they were relatively expensive

[3] Chase, *Greeting Cards*, p. 21.

to purchase, Prang cards involved not fewer than eight colors and sometimes as many as twenty. His carefully printed lithographs were further enhanced by the quality of his artists. Prang had a special love for nature and especially for florals. He hired the best artists of the day to depict the scenes and still lifes of his cards. The designs were always tasteful and refined, and the sentiments, when included, were minimal. Usually a short phrase from a poem by Longfellow or Tennyson was sufficient.

Not entirely by coincidence, the retirement of Louis Prang in 1890 was followed by the longest downward turn in the history of the business.

1900 AND AFTER

Gibson and Company were distributing German-made cards by 1880, and began producing their own cards soon after that. The depression that rocked the country in 1895 had a major effect on the infant greeting card industry, but by 1900 things were beginning to change. The card industry really emerged as a major force during the years between the turn of the century and World War I. By 1900 Gibson had incorporated and Alfred Bartlett began making first-rate cards in Boston.

In 1906, Fred Winslow Rust opened a bookshop and gift store in Kansas City. He began by collecting Prang cards but soon started to print his own in the back of his store. His first Christmas card was also this country's first *enveloped* card and the first *frenchfold* card as well. Rust moved to Boston in 1908 to found Rust Craft Publishers, and continued to be the first in many areas of the card industry. He is credited with the first Valentine, Easter (1908), Thanksgiving, anniversary, bon voyage (1912), birthday, and braille cards.

Also in 1906, Jacob Sapirstein began his horse-drawn jobbing business in Cleveland, later to become American Greetings. A year later, Sidney J. Burgoyne and Sons was founded in Philadelphia and Paul Volland in Chicago. In 1910 a young clerk named Joyce C. Hall moved from Norfolk, Nebraska, to Kansas City to begin wholesale jobbing of postcards and engraved Christmas cards. His older brother, R. B. Hall, joined him a year later. The Hall brothers' first business was completely destroyed by a fire in 1915. A local banker helped them regroup and start producing their own designs. W. F. Hall

but in Cincinnati he decided to turn over the family business, a French-made litho press, to his four youngest sons. Their first printing shop opened in 1853, and within six years the Gibsons were involved in a wide variety of printing, from business cards to perfume labels.

In 1880, Gibson and Company began to distribute German-made Christmas cards. Soon after, they began producing their own designs. Over the next decade, the company became so firmly established that it not only survived the Great Depression of the 1890s, but made considerable progress as well. Gibson Girl fashions were the rage, and the company incorporated as The Gibson Art Company. Around this time, Elizabeth Gordon's verse "Somebody Cares" became a national slogan, and 500,000 copies were sold in one year.

During the Roaring Twenties Gibson moved again to larger quarters and grew to include some 1,300 employees, with 150,000,000 greeting cards produced each year.

In the 1950s, Buzza Cardozo was acquired in Cal-

joined his brothers in 1920, and the Hallmark logo was introduced in 1923. Shortly thereafter, Hallmark introduced the first decorated gift wraps. Cards, however, remained the company's mainstay well into the 1940s.

Many families were separated by the war during 1917–1918, and cards became a means of communicating with those away. After the war, the economy began to boom, and cards have sold consistently well ever since. During the intervening years, they have proven to be both depression- and recession-proof. Many related paper products were introduced during the 1940s and 1950s. During the next two decades, many small card publishers emerged, and the majority have survived to the present. Today, the card industry is larger and more widely dispersed than ever before.

Profile: Gibson Greeting Cards, Inc.

This first profile honors the oldest card company in the world, Gibson, an American institution in printing that dates back to 1850 when George Gibson first came from England. George made it as far as St. Louis, ifornia and the company changed its name to Gibson Greeting Cards, Inc. The product lines were expanded to include party goods and candles. The Buzza line of cards is still a handsome offering today (see Figure 1-4) and helps give Gibson some of its great depth.

In 1964, Gibson was purchased by C.I.T. Financial Corporation, and in the 1980s C.I.T. was taken on by R.C.A. Today, Gibson sales amount to over $80 million per year. Most of the artwork is done by its large in-house staff; freelance work is available to the public.

Gibson has been a major force in the industry for more than a century, making it the oldest surviving (and thriving) card company throughout the world. Today, the Gibson image is far-reaching, from Jim Davis's great creations of Garfield the Cat to the ever popular sentiments of Kirby's Koalas. There is one thing that ties the Gibson family of cards together—quality.

A Twentieth Century Outline

1906   Fred Rust opens shop in Kansas City.

American Greetings founded in Cleveland.

Keating Company opens in Philadelphia.

1907   Burgoyne and Sons of Philadelphia founded.

1908   First Easter card introduced by Fred Rust after moving to Boston.

Gibson Art Company and P. F. Volland Company founded.

First Mothers Day service held by Miss Amma Jarvis of Philadelphia.

Figure 1-5
By Kate Whittaker. Copyright by and courtesy of Renaissance Greeting Cards, Springvale, Maine.

1910   Hall Brothers incorporate in Kansas City.

Mrs. John Bruce Dodd petitions for Fathers Day in Spokane, Washington.

1911   First get-well cards introduced by The Sunshine Society in western Massachusetts.

Friendship cards by Volland Company.

First sympathy designs.

1912   Fred Rust publishes first St. Patrick's Day and bon voyage cards.

1913   Rust Craft Publishers opens doors on India Street, Boston, and makes first thank-you cards.

1914   Jane and Arthur Norcross found Norcross Inc. on Fifth Avenue, New York City, and publish first personal greetings.

Second Sunday in May officially proclaimed Mothers Day.

1919   P. F. Volland assassinated in a private conference by a mentally ill woman because of a publication dispute.

1920   National Association of Greeting Card Publishers begins first advertising campaign.

Rust Craft moves to 100 Washington Street, Boston.

1922   Hallmark grows from a 4-person operation to a 120-person operation.

First graduation cards by Rust Craft.

1923   Hallmark introduces decorated gift wraps.

1920s & 1930s   Introduction of lined envelopes, gift wraps, novelty cards, cutouts, pop-ups, and die-cut cards.

1936   Hallmark moves to six-story building in Kansas City.

1940   Embossed cards are introduced.

1947   Sidney Burgoyne dies.

1949   Fred Rust dies.

1950s   Hallmark advertising sets new standards.

Hallmark Hall of Fame brought to television.

1955   Rust Craft moves to Dedham, Massachusetts, and opens largest card plant in the world.

1964   Gibson purchased by C.I.T. Financial Corporation.

1970s   Birth of many small card companies throughout the country.

1971   Recycled Paper Products started by Philip Friedman and Michael Keiser.

1975   Renaissance Greeting Cards founded.

1981   Norcross and Rust Craft merge; Rust Craft moves to Westchester, Pennsylvania.

1982   Rust Craft discontinues making cards.

American Greetings buys Rust Craft of Canada.

Today   *Hallmark* is the largest card company in the world, with an estimated annual sales of $1 billion. Hallmark is still a privately owned company, based in Kansas City, and it produces approximately 18,000 new designs each year.

American Greetings is clearly the other dominant force in the industry, with 17,000 employees in 24 plants throughout the world. American Greetings produces an estimated 12,000 original designs a year. Its headquarters are still in Cleveland.

Gibson celebrated its 125th anniversary in 1975. It is one of the top five companies in sales and is still located in Cincinnati.

Recycled Paper Products has grown into one of the nation's top four companies. It is based in Chicago and is still growing at a phenomenal pace.

The other top card publishers are Paramount, Charmcraft, Drawing Board Inc., and Sidney J. Borgoyne and Sons.

The National Association of Greeting Card Publishers estimated that in 1980 over 7 billion cards were sold—approximately half of all the personal mail sent during that year.

CARD TRENDS

Trends are inevitably tied to public opinion and acceptance. Whenever possible, publishers like to set new trends, but working within the framework of preestablished public tastes is considerably safer. Predicting what might sell is risky business, so caution is the general rule. New ideas are normally slipped in with older ones. In this way, trends and styles do develop, but at a safe pace.

By the 1950s the majority of card types had been invented. Intricate folds, die cuts, and various forms of ornamentation were already competing for attention in the market. From the early days when cards were handmade came many of the ingenious ways of making cards. These were added to newer printing methods of embossing and stamping to produce cards that were even more embellished. Publishers regard ornamentation as a way of adding *value* to a design, and during the 1960s some of the fanciest cards of all time were published.

By the time I entered the field, much of this was at a high point. Most cards came to me requiring some type of bake or leaf and an insert or inside spot design. Many cards had multiple applications. The most dreaded single application was glitter; for my colleagues and me, everything about glitter seemed distasteful. Besides choosing a color and glueing down the glitter, the final discouragement was the realization that we were covering up our own work. Aesthetically, the days of glitter and fluorescent colors were low points for many of us.

Figure 1-6
By Tom Cante (signed G. Willikers). Used by permission of Norcross-Rust Craft Divisions of Windsor Communications Group, Inc.

Another trend of the 1960s was filling up the surface with positive areas of design and ornamentation. Details and embellishments covered almost the entire front of many cards. The use of negative space was at an all-time minimum. *Note*: Positive area and positive space traditionally refer to the lights and darks within the central subject of a design. All surrounding areas not part of the subject are considered negative space.

In terms of technique, the 1960s and early 1970s saw many different varieties of form and style. The most generally accepted form was the *painterly* method of applying opaque colors with visible strokes. This was done in two basic ways: the loose *wash* and the heavier *impasto* technique. Impasto refers to the method of layering on pigments to simulate oil painting. Often, these styles were handled with great proficiency, but today they look noticeably old-fashioned. These old-fashioned styles are still popular with a few com-

Figure 1-7
Horses, circa 1960. This design with its use of heavy opaque gouache is typical of the *painterly* card styles of the 1960s. Used by permission of Norcross-Rust Craft Divisions of Windsor Communications Group, Inc.

Figure 1-8
Wedding Wishes. The new *graphics* look of the 1970s replaced the *painterly* styles of the 1960s. The dark blue background was also an innovation at the time. Courtesy Hallmark Cards, Inc.

panies, some of which are trying to recreate a nostalgic past and some that simply like the appeal of the painterly style.

In a general sense, the 1970s underwent another change in styles. The painterly look began to give way to a newer graphic look, in which the designs became more two-dimensional or flat than the three-dimensional look of earlier cards. Cards also became less crowded and busy-looking. More negative space appeared, and, for the first time on a large scale, verses were less evident; they even disappeared altogether in some designs.

These new changes opened up a whole new look in cards. Hallmark, a leader of this trend, became more and more comfortable with a simple yet dignified format. Other companies fol-

lowed, including some that belonged to a new class of publishers: the small shop-oriented businesses that began to crop up in New England and along the East Coast and West Coast. By the 1980s, these smaller companies were going strong, and their influence on the market has strengthened the industry tremendously. This has been done through the variety of cards and by the high quality of the new designs.

In some ways, these smaller publishers filled in the spaces the larger companies did not cover for a variety of reasons. Some types of cards were too risky and others were simply not universal enough to market nationwide. So the smaller manufacturers stepped in to fill this void by producing locally oriented cards and cards that celebrated minor occasions. Very general cards were

Figure 1-9
By Kate Whittaker, inside: *"To someone who had it all and still has a little left, Happy Birthday."* The 1980s has brought with it a more casual type of message. Copyright by and courtesy of Renaissance Greeting Cards, Springvale, Maine.

introduced as well. These were designs with no specific message other than of people communicating with one another.

Today, we can buy cards in many places. The shopping malls have spread out over the U.S. and Europe and have brought many "small" designs with them. We can now buy cards not only in drugstores and dime stores, but also in gift shops, bookstores, and specialty shops of all kinds.

It is uncertain how much the competition between large and small card publishers over-laps, but thanks to the overall world economy, greeting cards remain a basic value and the market seems safe enough for both to live in.

What about the future? What is the next trend likely to be? Perhaps the key to the future lies in the past. What often seems so new and avant garde is really a combination of old and new ideas put together. No artist has ever set the world in a totally new direction without some help from the past. In any case, the newest cards are the ones we are about to produce. We are the deciding factor.

Chapter Two

Drawing and Color

Figure 2-1 This beautiful design by Michael DiGiorgio is as much a wildlife painting as it is a greeting card. In fact, the artist is both a card designer and a wildlife illustrator. Courtesy of the artist.

Over the past few years, I have looked at many portfolios. While at Rust Craft, I occasionally reviewed prospective employees for the art director. My function was not to hire artists, but to screen applicants at the initial interview. If a portfolio was strong, I set up an appointment for a further interview with an art director or the creative director. If a portfolio was weak, I tried to give advice on what might be added or deleted before the person reapplied.

Currently, I look at portfolios, in my capacity as a teacher, in a much more relaxed fashion.

The following conclusions on the general needs of card and paper artists is based on my own experiences and is not meant to be all-inclusive.

THE NEED FOR GOOD DRAWING

Perhaps the most important aspect of a good portfolio is good, solid drawing. The creative director at Rust Craft had instructed me to look at portfolios without regard for art degrees, former employment, and the like.

Figure 2-2
Make a Joyful Noise. Good drawing is the foundation of every good card. Reprinted with the permission of Gibson Greeting Cards, Inc., with all rights reserved.

I was told that if a person could draw, a sixth-grade education was sufficient. I did not take this literally, but it does point out the director's attitude concerning the need to draw well. Good drawing is essential to most commercial art fields and particularly to greeting cards. Some artists may only need to draw well relative to cartooning or certain product rendering, but most card artists need to be able to render a variety of subjects convincingly.

A good color sense, on the other hand, can be learned on the job. To a certain extent, most artists go through at least some degree of color reorientation when hired either full-time or part-time.

Returning to drawing, the key to being successful in cards centers around the ability to render different subjects convincingly, whether

figure, floral, scenic, or whatever. Versatility will go a long way toward keeping you busy.

My first experience as a greeting card designer was in florals, and I was surprised to discover how much I did not know about my chosen subject. Over the years, I have collected book and magazine references, sketched from nature, photographed, and generally come to learn how flowers work, as well as how they look. Remember, many people who buy cards know the subjects well, and art directors count on you to match that knowledge.

Figure 2-3
Roses, by Ron Lister. Used by permission of Norcross-Rust Craft Divisions of Windsor Communications Group, Inc.

In summation, good eye and hand control, knowledge of your subjects, and visible proof you can draw correctly are all essential to a solid card portfolio.

COLOR

Almost all commercial artists develop some sort of color sense over the years. Most of us have a favorite assortment of hues we presume to call our own, but it is difficult to sort out just how we have arrived at these selections. We are subject to countless varieties of color through various media, and our senses cannot help but be influenced by at least some outside stimuli. Being conscious of our surroundings helps us to be aware of where our choices come from when we choose one color over another.

When I reviewed portfolios at Rust Craft, I was able to identify certain schools and even certain classes by what I saw. Special problems in color, such as drawing an expressionist *fantastic bird*, were often similar in color palette and form, even though the exercise was clearly developed for the students to express themselves individually. For instance, violet and yellow were often used to answer this problem. The students in the fantastic bird exercise, while trying to give an original and subjective treatment to their drawings, often turned out designs that were neither as original nor as individual as they believed. The point is that we quite often confuse what is objective in color with what is subjective and vice versa.

As commercial designers, we must contend with the objective or universal aspects of color, more than we have to when painting for ourselves. Publishers know what media and colors photograph the best. They also have an idea of which colors will sell and which ones will not. In fine arts, for example, we do not have to consider quite as many things when we paint. We are free to use second- and third-degree colors at will, but these same colors are too dirty, too muddy, for most greeting card work. Cards are, for the most part, clean and tidy. Even shadows and neutral tones are kept relatively pure. For most of us, this means we have to adjust our color range when we work commercially. We become more conscious of color harmony and universal colors.

Color Harmony

Color harmony is in most cases a sought-after effect. There may be occasions when jolting the viewer is desired. Certain label designs, such as candy bar wrappers, are created to bring quick attention to the product, rather than to create a harmonious feeling. Some cards are likewise not very pleasing to the eye, but, in general, it can be assumed that harmonious coloration is a chief aim.

Many of us learn about color relationships in courses at school or through books that rely on color theories. The simplest color theories involve schematic interpretations of colors and their relationships. The most common one is the twelve-hued color wheel (Figure 2-4), which revolves around the three *primaries*: red, yellow, and blue. Mixtures of the primary colors give the remaining *secondary* and *tertiary* hues. With each mixture, colors become weaker. Thus, the secondary color orange is weaker than any of the primaries, and the tertiary colors yellow-orange and blue-violet are weaker still. The twelve-hued wheel gives us a ready-made chart for producing harmonious colors. In his great book, *The Art of Color*, Johannes Itten tells us, "The color combinations called 'harmonious' in common speech usually are composed of closely similar chromas, or else different colors in the

Figure 2-4
The twelve-hued *color wheel.*

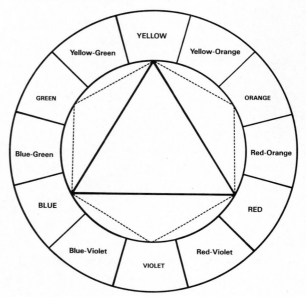

same shades. They are combinations of colors that meet without sharp contrast. As a rule, the assertion of harmony or discord simply refers to an agreeable-disagreeable . . . scale. Such judgments are personal sentiments without objective force. The concept of color harmony should be removed from the realm of subjective attitude into that of objective principle. Harmony implies balance, symmetry of forces."[1]

This balance is created naturally by our eyes under specific conditions. When we are confronted with only the color green for an extended length of time, we will see red (green's complementary) when we close our eyes or look away from the green object. Complementary colors are found opposite each other on the color wheel. Thus, if we stare at an orange shape for some time and close our eyes, the after-image we see will be blue. This reaction is caused by fatigue of the color receptors in our eyes.

When we mix complementaries on paper, we get gray. It is medium gray that gives our eyes equilibrium and allows them to relax. So any combination of colors that yields medium gray will help balance our colors. Note that complementary pairs are really mixtures of the three primaries: red and green (blue and yellow); orange (red and yellow) and blue; and so on. Essentially, this includes any mixture that contains enough of the three primaries to yield middle gray.

A simple but effective color harmony based on color chords of two, three, and four tones (*dyads, triads,* and *tetrads*) has been devised by Itten (see Figure 2-5). These revolving triangles and rectangles can be placed in any position and still yield harmonious relationships.

Specific color relations appear throughout this book, but learning about objective color principles can help guide us. These principles are not meant to dictate to us how to paint. Our subjective senses will guide us the majority of the time. It is only when we need a little help that conscious reference to such color schemes should be relied upon.

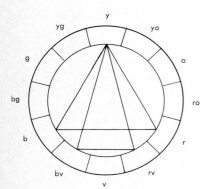

COLOR HARMONY
AND VARIATIONS

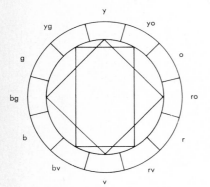

Figure 2-5
Color harmony. This system, devised by Johannes Itten, shows a simple formula for mixing harmonious colors. Any use of the colors represented by these geometric shapes (in any position) yields gray. Courtesy Van Nostrand Reinhold Co., New York, New York.

VERSATILITY

Being versatile is naturally helpful to any artist, but in the card field it is perhaps more pronounced than in other types of commercial art. This applies especially to those working or freelancing full-time. The card market is very diverse, with the large companies producing a wide range of styles and subjects. It is a misconception to believe one particular personal style will suffice. Only the very best artists can rely on just a single look. Designing and marketing your own cards is one way to circumvent this. The only other method of being successful with just one type of card is to find several companies that are happy with your style. This takes time and effort, but it can be done.

The basic reality of the situation is a little different. Most companies prefer to assign each particular design. This is done to avoid duplication. If a general rule applies, it is that larger companies are most likely to be specific about assignments. They tend to control subjects and treatments very carefully because of the greater risks of duplication involved. Smaller companies may be more concerned with the artist main-

[1] Johannes Itten, *The Art of Color* (Van Nostrand Reinhold Company, 1973), p. 21.

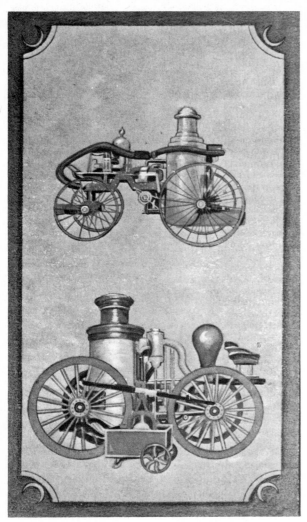

Figure 2-6

Antique fire engines. Although primarily a floral and landscape artist at Rust Craft, the author often painted other types of cards. This one was done for Australia. Used by permission of Norcross-Rust Craft Divisions of Windsor Communications Group, Inc.

take notice of unusual or dissimilar appearances. A variation in technique or medium will help to land a few jobs along the way.

As a final note, not all companies work year-round. Smaller ones often close shop for a few weeks or even months until the next year's designs start again. Even large publishers have slow periods of production, and it is usually the less versatile artists who are affected the most.

ASSESSING THE SITUATION

The card and paper product market is a wide-open and highly competitive field. Breaking into it takes some time, and staying in it takes patience, but there is a constant mobility of artists within the field. Some artists move on to other related fields, say, illustration or advertising. Others move up or down the corporate ladder, taking jobs off the board. So, even though the competition is stiff, jobs are constantly being made available.

In freelancing, breaking in has its own set of problems. Freelance artists normally work on their own, and the problems that arise are made somewhat more difficult because of this. Loneliness and insecurity are fairly common among freelance artists. Patience is truly a virtue in this branch of cardmaking. Building up clientele and maintaining relations by telephone and mail are not easy tasks.

More specific problems and assessments will be discussed throughout the book, but start doing some of the necessary footwork now. Search out companies that already produce cards similar to your own tastes. Contact these places and try to keep in touch with them. Make lists of all the good card stores in your area. Become familiar with which brands are sold. Use the telephone book to find local showrooms, distributors, and retailers. The more you know about the general and local markets, the better the chances are of making the right choices and decisions.

taining the company's image than with the possibility of duplicating subject and format.

Most companies' outputs follow a basic yearly plan, a pattern dominated by holidays, special occasions, and seasonal everyday cards. An event like Christmas may tie up a large portion of a publisher's output for several months at a stretch, during which time few everyday cards may be called for. Anyone not capable of handling specific Christmas subjects and treatments may find work hard to come by until the designing season is over.

Besides being versatile with different subjects, it is also helpful to be able to work with different media. Different subjects often call for different treatments, and companies normally

Profile:
Victor Sindoni,
Former Art Director

Victor Sindoni started art classes at the age of ten. After graduating from the Massachusetts College of Art in the 1930s, he went to work for Rust Craft

Figure 2-7
Linocut Angel, by Victor Sindoni. Courtesy of the artist.

Publishers as a board artist. He eventually became an art director, a position he held for nearly twenty years. Mr. Sindoni is now retired and has returned to painting for himself. I began my interview by asking him what the functions of an art director are.

Victor. Basically, what you do is direct a group of people. The company always wanted me to teach the artist to draw, but I always thought that was wrong. Artists should know their craft. What you do is to direct. Tell them what flavor you want in a particular drawing. Or you might give a general criticism, whether it's too heavy or it needs a little more color. But basically, if you have got four or five individuals, you know what each one can do best and you feed along that line.

Ron. What did you look for in a portfolio?

Victor. We looked for good drawing, good color, and good layout. Educational background doesn't mean a row of beans, as far as I'm concerned. What I-we wanted was in the portfolio.

Ron. In terms of drawing and color, what did you specifically look for?

Victor. Techniques. In greeting cards especially you need a number of techniques. You have to be fairly versatile because there's not enough of each type of design to sustain. With colors, we look for a fairly clean, bright design, as contrasted to fine arts.

Ron. After a new person was hired, how did you treat that person?

Victor. What I used to do was to give the person a couple of weeks to play around and get used to the feeling. I used to have to fight the company about this. I didn't expect anything for at least two weeks. Some companies don't expect anything for two or three months.

Ron. What advice do you have for anyone getting into full-time card designing?

Victor. What I usually tell people, if they haven't had much experience, is to go to a greeting card store and look at all types of cards and get a flavor, and then see what they like. Whatever it is, they should lean on what they like. Work on that. Once they learn how to do one thing well, then it is easier to diversify. It takes a while to learn the ropes. I knew people who worked for two years, and we didn't know whether to keep them or not. And then finally something would happen and they would turn around and start doing great work.

Chapter Three

Materials

Figure 3-1 Courtesy of Anatoly Dverin.

For a commercial designer, the use of first-rate materials is essential. We are all limited, to an extent, by the quality of the tools and materials we choose. Any deviation from using the best equipment possible should be avoided. Even practicing new techniques or media should be done with the best materials.

There are substantial differences in the quality of goods made by various manufacturers. Even some of the best companies offer *student* brand lines, which are inferior to their top lines.

Take these matters seriously. This guide will make some suggestions as to certain brand names; however, some of these materials may be available in my area but not in yours. Take it upon yourself to determine the quality of materials available to you. Many of my students have been sold inferior products, often at top prices. Good advice is not always to be had from art stores, so caution is recommended.

This section includes all the basic papers, boards, and films used in card and paper design, but will not include either printing or photographic papers.

BOARDS

Board and board-type papers are the most widely used surfaces in paper design. They are heavy, durable, and able to handle a wide range of me-

STRATHMORE.

14 LB. TRACING
9" X 12" 50 Sheets

Tracing Designed for professional designers who need to use a good tracing paper.

Strathmore 300 SERIES Colored Art Paper
9" X 12" 40 sheets

Colored Art Paper
This is a good quality construction paper. It's great for drawing, coloring, block printing, silk screening, or cutting up into designs. Each package comes in a variety of rich and brilliant colors.

13 LB. LAYOUT BOND
11" X 14" 50 Sheets

Layout Bond Natural white vellum paper is made especially for designers.

Strathmore 500 Charcoal

Charcoal This 100% cotton fiber paper has a traditional laid pattern and provides the proper resistance for precise shading with charcoal and pastels. The raised texture makes it a fascinating paper for all mediums.

Strathmore 300 SERIES Bristol wt. Board
SMOOTH 11" X 14" 20 Sheets

Bristol Weight Board An economical, heavyweight paper in a choice of two surfaces. Smooth is ideal for fine pen and ink, pencil, mechanical drawing. Vellum is designed for a broad range of drawing and painting including crayon, pencil, charcoal, watercolor and art markers.

Sketch

Strathmore 400
9"x12" 100 sheets

Sketch This is a general purpose sketch paper for classroom, experimentation, or perfecting technique with pen, pencil and a variety of other media. Rugged spiral wire binding makes it ideal for field use.

Bristol

Strathmore 400
11"x18" 15 sheets

Bristol Bristol weights of drawing paper have all the characteristics of a fine drawing surface in a heavier weight sheet. It comes in a smooth surface suited for pen or pencil, and a vellum surface ideal for a broad range or media.

Other Artist Paper

Illustration Board
100% Cotton Fiber Mounted on both sides of illustration board. It creates a balanced tension that prevents warping. Highest quality illustration board available.

Regular Surface		
240-1	20"x30"	Hvy. Wt.
240-3	22"x30"	Lt. Wt.
240-4	30"x40"	Hvy. Wt.
High Surface		
240-2	20"x30"	Hvy. Wt.
240-5	30"x40"	Hvy. Wt.

Figure 3-2
Strathmore boards and papers are among the best in the world. Nearly all the cards the author has done have been painted on Strathmore illustration board. Courtesy Strathmore Paper Co., Westfield, Massachusetts.

dia. These surfaces come in fairly standard sizes ranging from 15" × 20" to as large as 40" × 60".

Strathmore Illustration Board

Strathmore makes the best-quality board available. It is made of 100 percent rag (cotton fiber) facing papers (outside surfaces), bonded and separated by middles of high-grade white stock. This board is double-faced and can be split in two if desired. The surface is available in two finishes: high (smooth) and regular (slight texture). Both are of the highest quality, but I have found the regular superior for painting media. Sizes run 20" × 30" and 30" × 40" and can be purchased in packages of ten and twenty-five. Individual sheets are available, generally at higher prices.

Strathmore board is very strong. It takes all wet media well and does not buckle under normal use. The board is also excellent for reworking and erasing. Lesser boards will not handle reworking without showing negative effects.

Strathmore board is the most commonly used surface in the business and is used by illustrators and architects as well.

Strathmore Drawing Board

The Strathmore drawing board is also 100 percent rag. It is technically a paper, but has board characteristics. It comes in two finishes: medium and high, and in five different weights. The weights range from one ply ($1/125''$) to five ply ($1/32''$). The high surface is smooth and is excellent for pen-and-pencil work. The medium finish, which has a slight texture, will take almost any medium. Sizes are 23" × 29" and 30" × 40".

These paper boards have the same advantages as the illustration board, and are essentially the same surface, minus the middle stock. The one- and two-ply surfaces have the look and feel of a very tough paper and have the reworking and erasing characteristics of board.

The middle, or medium, surface has a slight grain I find well-suited for charcoals and pastels as well as watercolor.

Bainbridge No. 80 Illustration Board

Bainbridge No. 80 is a quality material. It is a medium-grained, *cold-press* surface, suitable for dry media. It comes in two thicknesses ($1/16''$ and $3/32''$). The double thickness is better for reworking and erasing. Sizes and packages vary. The single-thickness sheets come twenty-five and fifty to a package and vary in size from 15" × 20" to 30" × 40". Double thicknesses come twelve and twenty-five per package in the same dimensions.

Note: Cold-press paper is created by pressing the paper fibers with cold rollers into various thicknesses. It leaves the surface porous and semitextured. Hot-pressed papers have a smoother and less porous surface than cold-pressed papers. They are not as well suited for transparent watercolor, but are employed for opaque techniques and other drawing purposes.

Bainbridge No. 172 Illustration Board

Bainbridge No. 172 is a *hot-press* board with a very smooth surface. It is made especially for lettering and fine-line work in pen and ink. It also comes in single and double thicknesses and is sold in the same dimensions and quantities as the No. 80 board. It has reasonably good reworking qualities.

Bainbridge No. 90 Illustration Board

The 90S is a smooth surface board. The 90R has a fairly rough texture. The smooth board is best for pen and ink; the textured board accepts charcoals, pencils, pastels, and watercolors. This board is single thickness, however, and is not capable of taking much reworking. It comes in 20″ × 30″ and 30″ × 40″ sheets.

Note: All Bainbridge boards are one-sided sheets mounted on a plain back surface for weight and strength.

Strathmore Series 400 Bristol Board

Strathmore Series 400 is a fine board for general use. It comes in vellum, which has a slight tooth, and in a smooth finish. Sheets are more limited for color media, but good otherwise, especially for pen and ink techniques. It is 100 percent rag as well, which means it will not deteriorate with age. It is available in 22″ × 30″ sheets only.

Bristol Pads

Bristol pads are normally sold in two-ply and three-ply sheets with twenty to thirty sheets per pad. The surfaces vary from smooth to slightly textured. They offer a harder surface than illustration boards and are generally good for most media. Erasing qualities vary from average to good, but beware of student-quality pads.

Prelined Bristol and Illustration Boards

Several companies make good-quality boards with a nonreproducible blue grid built in. The grid has every inch mark accentuated for easy viewing. On the average, there are eight lines to the inch. These sheets are approximately 22″ × 28″ in diameter, although some are sold in a smaller pad form.

Other Brands

There are several companies retailing illustration boards on the East Coast. The Charrette Corporation sells top-quality materials with their own name as well as others. They are located in New York, Boston, New Haven, and Cambridge. They also offer a complete line of supplies for designers, drafters, and architects.

Another brand on the East Coast is Superior, which sells 100 percent rag illustration boards in both hot- and cold-press.

PAPER

Watercolor Papers

I have used watercolor paper on relatively few commercial designs. Illustration board has proven far more suitable. It accepts watercolor and gouache quite well, and it has great reworking and erasing qualities. Watercolor papers are not particularly good for corrective work, although they do offer some unique effects. Watercolor paper is very porous. The watermarks and uneven textures give it a quality quite dissimilar from illustration board. Colors bleed and dry in strikingly different ways. So for some special effects, I can recommend watercolor paper.

Slightly toothed or smooth surfaces are the most serviceable. I have nothing against rough papers, but card designing is normally done to size or, at the most, scaled up one-and-a-half times. This is really too small an area to take advantage of rough paper. At such a scale, fine details and tight control are difficult to obtain.

Generally, hot-press papers are somewhat less serviceable for cards. Pigments do not sink into the surface exceptionally well or evenly. Building color mixtures may be more difficult,

Figure 3-3
This swan design was painted around 1950. Watercolor paper was used, and the design was later reduced by one-third.

but only by experimenting will you find if they are effective for you or not.

Cold-press papers are typically more expensive than hot-press, but I prefer them for their absorbent qualities.

Good watercolor papers are 100 percent rag, but remembering that commercial work is photographed in a fairly short period, I am not certain they are a necessity.

The best papers are Arches from France and Fabriano from Italy. These and other quality companies carry a watermark trademark on the front of their papers to indicate which side to paint on, although the reverse side can be used as well.

Finally, some of the very best papers are handmade and have inconsistencies in the fibers. Many watercolor artists find this attractive because it adds a touch of the unexpected to each painting, but under normal circumstances, the unexpected is not what a commercial artist appreciates.

Strathmore Artist Watercolor Paper

Strathmore Artist watercolor paper is 100 percent cotton fiber. It is mold-made and comes in three surfaces: cold-press, hot-press, and rough grain. Standard weights of 72 lbs. and 140 lbs. are sold, but not 300 lbs. The hot-press is good for pen and ink, and the cold-press is very good for color. Sheets are 22″ × 30″ and are sold in blocks of twenty-five or separately. Prices are the same for all three surfaces.

Arches Watercolor Paper

A fine 100 percent handmade rag paper, Arches watercolor paper comes in cold-press and rough and in three weights: 90 lbs., 140 lbs., and 300 lbs. The two lighter-weight cold-press papers are strong and durable. They can be used for all watercolor techniques and will take some reworking. The 300 lb. weight papers are quite expensive. Their cost may be three-and-a-half times that of a 90 lb. stock, and though they accept more pigment than lighter-weight papers, I am not sure they are needed for card designing. One advantage they do have, however, is that if the surface is kept reasonably dry, a 300 lb. paper may not need to be stretched. Sheets are 22″ × 30″.

Note: Lighter-weight watercolor papers are wetted first on both sides. They are then wiped clean of excess water and laid on a flat, preferably wooden, surface. The paper is then taped down with water-soluble tape, by overlapping the paper and the mounting surface. Two- or two-and-a-half-inch wide tape is normally used. When the paper dries, it stretches completely flat and is ready for painting.

Fabriano Artistico Watercolor Paper

Another great 100 percent rag paper, Fabriano Artistico watercolor paper is mold-made. It is available in rough, cold-press, and hot-press. The rough paper may be too rough for card designs. The sheets are 22″ × 30″ and come in three weights: 90 lbs., 147 lbs., and 300 lbs.

OTHER PAINTING SURFACES

There are no rules governing what surfaces to work on. Drawing papers, charcoal papers, colored art papers, pastel papers, and even parchments can be used. Most of these different papers will accept some degree of wet media if they are properly mounted. In fact, the first card I ever designed was painted on a plain brown washtowel mounted on illustration board (see Figure 10-6 and Plate 4).

Mounted Papers

Rubber cement is one of the basic means of mounting papers. To ensure it will not buckle when wet, coat both the back of the paper and the front of the mounting surface. When both are completely dry, they can be placed together. Usually, a piece of tracing or lightweight paper is inserted between the two cemented surfaces.

The third paper is then slipped carefully out as the two surfaces are brought together. This ensures the paper and mounting surface will not come together prematurely or unevenly during the process.

Premounted papers are also available. The Crescent Board Company mounts a variety of Strathmore colored papers onto a heavy stock. The surfaces are smooth or slightly textured. Some of the more neutral colors do not reproduce well, tending to come out a little "dirty." For this reason, I recommend using only the cleanest colors and smooth surfaces for art that is to be reproduced.

Wood-Grained Papers

These are actual wood veneer strips, sometimes made of oak. They are sold in thin sheets which can be cut and mounted easily (see Figure 3-4).

Figure 3-4
For Nephew, by Ron Lister. This design was painted directly on a mounted wood grain paper. The wood veneer was first stained with gouache. Note that the grain of the wood was integrated into the design. Used by permission of Norcross-Rust Craft Divisions of Windsor Communications Group, Inc.

Wood-grained paper stains very nicely and can be painted on with good effects. It accepts gouache better than transparent watercolor.

Tracing Papers

Used for everything from initial rough sketches and layouts to finished drawings ready for transferring, tracing paper is a necessity in card designing. It can be purchased in many sizes and forms, including a gridded format useful for precise measuring. These are especially helpful in cards with borders and label or title areas, as well as with gift wraps and other "repeated" type designs.

The price and quality of most papers is similar, whether bought in pads or in bulk.

Figure 3-5
Most cards are designed first on tracing paper. This drawing, by Ron Lister, was used to transfer gold leaf onto prepared acetate.

Canson and Montgolfier Tracing Papers

One of the world's greatest names in paper manufacturing, Canson and Montgolfier of France has been making fine papers for well over one hundred years. Tracing pads contain 50 sheets, and come in an assortment of weights: No. 50 medium, No. 90 extra heavy, and No. 110 super thick. All weights are very transparent. They each have a slight tooth, and contain no oil, leaving no odor. The heavier stocks can be worked on with a light wash.

Tracing Vellum

Generally used for engineering and technical drawings, vellums are strong, erasable, and translucent, but not transparent. They are used in presentations and mock-up designs, where colored overlays are used.

Vellums come in rolls, packages, and pads, and are slightly more expensive than tracing papers.

Cronaflex and Drafting Films

These films are designed for ink or pencil drawing techniques. They are one-sided, nonglare surfaces, usually made of polyester (see Figure 3-6).

Drafting films are most commonly used for overlays, but line plates can be made directly from them. Gray pencil work that is done directly on a design must be color separated for reproduction. This can cause blurring and thickening of the original line, but if the pencil is done on an overlay of cronaflex or a similar film, it can be used as a photo-ready mechanical, saving time and money. The major drawback is that the reproduced gray line tends to be totally achromatic in character, possessing little of the warmth of a color-separated line. One company I worked for stopped using films for this reason.

Transfer Papers

Artist transfer papers are used to transfer graphic designs and drawings from one surface (usually tracing paper) to another (usually illustration board). There are several types to choose from. On anything less than the darkest backgrounds,

Figure 3-6
This sketch, by Ron Lister, was drawn on Cronaflex film using a soft lead pencil.

I use the regular graphite transfer paper. When transferring onto very dark surfaces, I use white transfer. Yellow, blue, and red are also available, but as a card designer, I have had little use for them.

Note: Carbon transfer papers, like those used in typing, are not suitable for artwork. Only special artists' transfers leave a grease-free line that can be easily erased and will not smudge or blur.

Transfers come in 12″ × 12″ rolls or 18″ × 24″ sheets. Though they are relatively inexpensive, some designers choose to make their own. This is simple to do. Graphite shavings (like those that collect in a mechanical pencil sharpener) are mixed with a little turpentine and rubbed onto tracing paper with a paper towel. After the surface dries, excess graphite is then wiped from the surface. By controlling the amount of graphite used, lighter transfers can be made. Many artists prefer to make their own in order to control this aspect.

Frisket and Masking Films and Liquid Masks

These products are essentially the same. Both are used for masking off areas in order to paint around them, not over them.

Frisket comes in both liquid and paper film. The paper form is best for blocking out large areas such as borders and title panels. The liquid variety is better for detailed work and small, confined areas.

Note: Liquid frisket is applied with a watercolor brush. Be sure to saturate the brush first with soap and water. If the frisket dries directly on the brush, it will not be easy to remove and will likely destroy the point. I recommend using older brushes for the job.

Masking film/paper is laminated on a backing sheet. It is transparent, so the work underneath is left visible. The paper cuts easily and peels from the backing to expose a mild adhesive. It is placed on the board much like transparent tape is and then is ready to paint around or over. When the paint is dry, the paper peels off the board with little problem and should reveal a paint-free area.

Note: Frisket paper will lift off much of the drawing underneath it. Drawings which are to be covered with frisket, either liquid or paper, should be made especially heavy. Also, it is not good to put frisket over areas that are already painted. It may or may not lift the paint beneath. Frisket paper and masking film are sold in rolls or by the sheet.

Figure 3-7
This cartoon, by Mike Rodgers, showing a hospital patient making a mobile out of his pill cups, was drawn and painted directly on acetate

Prepared Acetate

This refers to acetate (clear plastic) that has been treated on both sides with a gelatin layer. Prepared acetate will accept inks, watercolor, gouache, or dyes. It can be washed clean, except for dyes, which sink into the surface. This type of acetate is excellent for all types of overlay work, and is used quite often in graphic design.

Prepared acetate comes in rolls, pads, and packages, normally interleaved with black paper. Individual sheets are the most expensive.

Note: When used as overlays, all acetates cut out a little light from the surface underneath. Although they are only .005″ thick, each overlay can cut a small percentage of the light. Several overlays will make an underneath design slightly, but noticeably, darker.

Also, fingerprints will reduce the effectiveness of the acetate. Be sure to wipe clean all areas before working.

Untreated Acetate

These plastic sheets do not accept wet media. Water and ink will bead up when applied. Untreated acetates are used for covering finished artwork. They are less expensive than treated acetates and are normally interleaved with light blue paper to distinguish them from prepared acetates.

BRUSHES
Watercolor Brushes

Red sable brushes, from the tail of the Kolinsky, are the most uniform, versatile, and preferred brushes available. They are also getting to be very expensive. As a result, Sabeline (ox hair) and camel's hair brushes are becoming more popular. I still use only sable and believe it is better to limit the quantity rather than the quality of brushes used.

Winsor & Newton Series 7 Watercolor Brushes

Winsor & Newton still set the standard for sable brushes. Their tips are uniformly true and very durable. Flat-tipped brushes are not available in this series. Round tips come in standard sizes, with the smallest numbered 000 and the largest numbered 10. A No. 10 brush has a hair length of $1^1/4''$, while a 000 is $^7/32''$. A No. 10 brush costs over $100 retail, which is certainly a consideration. Because of the expense of top-quality brushes, most of us need to limit the number we work with. How large a selection is needed depends on several variables, including the scale, type, and techniques being used for the painting. I have an assortment of approximately two dozen brushes, ranging up to a No. 14 in size, but I use only a handful of these to do the majority of the work. Using good, well-kept brushes, I seldom have use for anything smaller than a No. 2 brush, though this certainly varies among designers. Likewise, a No. 6 brush is generally the largest brush I use for anything except backgrounds and very loose wash tones.

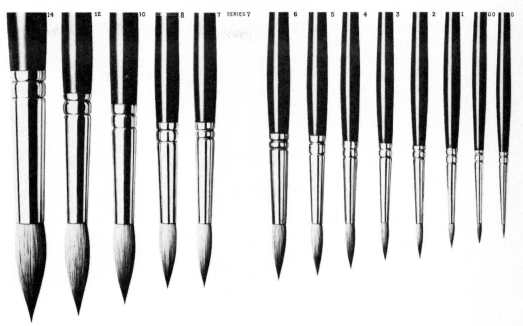

Figure 3-8
Winsor & Newton Series 7 water-color brushes are the finest quality available at any price. Courtesy Winsor & Newton, London, England.

Flat-Tipped Watercolor Brushes

Small flat-tipped brushes are normally used only for certain techniques and applications. Larger sizes are more common. These are used for painting large areas where uniform texture and pigment are required. They are also good for putting down large, quick wash tones where "fresh" strokes are necessary.

With flat brushes, sable is not a necessity, only an advantage.

Air Brushes

Air brushes are not as common as they once were in greeting card designing. Today they are used more in illustrations where larger formats are used. The cost of air brushes and air brush compressors, air regulators, and hoses can run quite high. Also, there are many models to choose from. If you are interested, do some serious comparison shopping to see what is available in your area.

Brush Care

With prices as high as they are, adequate care of brushes is a real concern. Watercolor brushes should never be allowed to stand with dry paint on them. All brushes should be washed thoroughly with mild soap and water after each use and placed in an upright position with the tip facing up. One option is to fill a jar with sand in which to keep the brushes free of one another. Whatever method you use, be sure not to let the brushes dry out with the tips bent or flattened by contact either with other brushes or with objects.

Good watercolor brushes should never be used with liquid mask, permanent inks, or any other product which is likely to destroy them. Instead, save your old brushes, and when the points have flattened out, put them to other uses.

COLOR MEDIA
Designers's Gouache

Of all the various color media available, designers' gouache is used the most. Combinations of gouache with watercolors, dyes, and other media are quite common, but it is the gouache itself that is most necessary to the designer or illustrator. Its most appreciated quality is in the opacity of the pigments. When used in normal concentrations, gouache has great covering power. Lighter colors can be successfully placed over darker ones, and many painterly techniques can be simulated. When thinned out, gouache reacts the same as watercolor paints, becoming clear and transparent. In this capacity, it is great for loose wash tones, which allow underlying colors to show through.

Designers' gouache is a relatively inexpensive paint medium, but it tends to harden faster and more permanently than watercolors. Some colors are also less durable than watercolors, and not all of the various pigments break down evenly when thinned out. In addition, some tend to become granular on the surface and are thus more difficult to use in smooth, transparent washes.

There are several student-quality brands of designers' gouache available, some of which are made by major companies. The quality seems to vary somewhat between brands, but as a general rule, they are still inferior products and should be considered as such.

Winsor & Newton Designers' Gouache

Winsor & Newton is an art supply manufacturer in England, that produces many of the very best materials available. Their designers' gouache and watercolor brushes are generally considered to be of the highest quality on the market.

In the past few years, many companies have lowered the quality of their paints in order to keep prices down, but not Winsor & Newton.

Their products tend to be more expensive than their competitors', but if results are measured, you are likely to get more for your money in the long run.

Winsor & Newton designers' gouache comes in medium-sized tubes (14 ml). There are four series as well as blacks and whites. The different series are marked one through four, and prices increase with the number. Series Four, which includes the cadiums, costs approximately two-and-a-half times as much as the Series One colors. There are thirty-five colors in the Series One group. Each tube lists color permanence on the back. The letter A stands for a good degree of permanence, the letter B for moderately fast to light, and the letter C for fugitive colors. Almost all the B's and C's appear in Series Two. Of the twenty-seven colors in Series Two, only twelve are permanent. Series Three and Four carry seven and eight tubes, respectively, all of which are marked A.

Those colors labeled C, such as Spectrum Violet, Peacock Blue, and Rose Tyrien, are highly fugitive, and many fade completely as time and light act upon them.

Recommended Gouache Colors

Here is a fairly complete list of the gouache colors I use most often. You may notice very few reds are to be found on this list. That is because I find the majority of red gouache colors are either

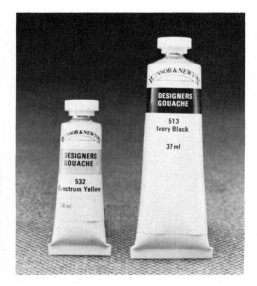

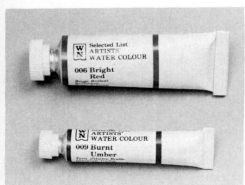

Figure 3-9
Also recommended are Winsor & Newton Designers gouache and watercolors. Courtesy of Winsor & Newton, London, England.

FINE ART MATERIALS SINCE 1832

too dirty or do not mix well with other colors. My solution to this has been to use watercolor reds instead of gouache reds, though only a few of these are suitable as well. They are listed under "Recommended Watercolors."

Yellows: Lemon Yellow (cool), Spectrum Yellow (closest to a primary yellow), Yellow Ochre (golden yellow), Marigold Yellow (light orange), Naples Yellow (yellow-white).

Oranges: Orange Lake Light (red-orange), Chinese Orange (brownish-orange).

Reds: Bengal Rose (a good cool red, but highly fugitive), Rose Carthame (a nice middle red, but not as good as the watercolor version).

Blues: Spectrum Violet (purple), Ultramarine Blue (closest to a primary blue), Sky Blue (a light middle-toned blue), Peacock Blue (warmer than sky), Turquoise Blue (blue-green).

Greens: Permanent Green Deep, Middle Green and Light Green (good clean greens), Olive Green (a favorite warm green).

Browns: Raw Sienna (red-brown), Burnt Sienna (darker), Ram Umber and Burnt Umber (cooler than Siennas). *Note*: The browns tend to dry out the fastest.

White: Zinc White (slightly yellowish), Permanent White.

Blacks: I prefer to mix black or to use Payne's Gray watercolor.

Note: There are approximately twice as many tubes of gouache available as are listed here. Some of your own favorites may not be included. I have attempted only to set a limited number of colors for those just starting out. I do use other colors myself, but the above list should provide a wide enough range that any colors not listed can be achieved through mixing.

Winsor & Newton Artists' Watercolors

Winsor & Newton Artists' Watercolors are made of the very best raw materials available. As a result, prices must be periodically adjusted to insure quality.

There are five series, marked AA (Permanent), A (Durable), and C (Fugitive). At present, 156 colors are available, the vast majority of which are AA's and A's.

Like many designers, I have a fairly large assortment of both designers' gouache and watercolors. Between the two, I can achieve a wide variety of effects while staying somewhat clear of the more fugitive colors.

Recommended Watercolors

With a choice of over 150 colors, it is difficult to set a limited number of recommended watercolors. In fact, most watercolors give good results. There are a few colors with very little covering power, such as sap green or hooker's green. Generally, however, most watercolors cover well enough, though not as opaquely as gouache colors.

The watercolors I value most are Rose Carthame and Permanent Rose. I believe Rose Carthame is the cleanest and purest warm red available. It mixes well and has good covering powers. Permanent Rose is perhaps the best cool red available. It is great for mixing purples and violets. Cadium Red is another fairly good warm red, but it is slightly muddy in comparison with Rose Carthame. I find the other reds, Scarlet Lake, Cadium Scarlet, Light Red, Winsor Red, andthe like to be muddy or dirty as well. They are good to use when mixing, but are not pure.

I especially like Payne's Gray, Davy's Gray, and Charcoal Gray for an assortment of warm and cool grays. Also of note: Winsor Emerald (a wonderfully cool green), Manganese Blue (similar to Peacock gouache but more permanent), Cerulean Blue (a beautifully clean light blue), and Olive Green (which is warmer than Olive Green gouache). You will have to do some exploring of your own to complete the list.

Bleed-Proof White

Several brands of bleed-proof white are available, including Luma and Dr. Martin's. They are all-purpose whites with good covering powers and designed not to bleed into other colors. *Note*: They will bleed if too much water is mixed in with them.

These nonbleed whites will not chip or peel on acetate and can be mixed with other colors if the need arises. One-ounce bottles are standard.

Luma and Dr. Martin's Watercolors (Dyes)

Luma and Dr. Martin's watercolors are liquid watercolors, highly concentrated and very brilliant at full strength. Luma makes eighty colors, while Dr. Martin's offers about fifty colors. Dr. Martin's also sells two sets of liquid paints: Dr. Martin's Synchromatic Transparent Watercolors, which are very transparent, and Dr. Martin's Radiant Concentrated Watercolors, which are slightly more brilliant and a little less transparent.

Luma comes in one-ounce bottles and Dr. Martin's in half-ounce bottles. Both brands are good quality.

Acrylics

Acrylics are the most widely used colors with a synthetic resin base. They are called *polymer colors* and are made by dispersing the pigments in an acrylic emulsion. The paint can be thinned with water, but when the surface dries (which is almost instantly), it leaves a hard film that is impervious to water. (See Figure 10-4, *Horses*, which was painted with acrylics.)

Acrylics can imitate a number of water-based media. They are nontoxic, nonallergenic, and very quick to manipulate. The latter quality makes them handy for artists who have little time and who seek high production.

Although the same pigments are used in acrylics as in other paints, the nature of the polymer is quite different in its appearance. The colors are brilliant, with a flexible, almost rubbery elasticity to them. They are too plastic for my own taste, but they do work well on large-scale jobs, such as large illustrations and posters. Generally, they are not well-suited for smaller jobs with a greeting card format. They do not blend or mix extremely well and do not photograph well at all. The colors tend to exhibit various degrees of translucency which are picked up by the camera. Flat color areas are most difficult with acrylics. Another drawback is plastic paints simply eat up brushes. They destroy the tips and hairs very quickly.

Oil-Based Paints

Oil-based paints are a favorite of mine, but not for commercial art. In fine arts, they are wonderfully controllable and are capable of achieving countless subtle effects. In commercial art, they are messy, toxic, and very slow to manipulate and dry. They are also difficult to photograph properly because of the glossiness of the surface and possible variations of thickness.

Occasionally, a publisher will make an exception and purchase work done in oils. Figure 7-9 shows an oil painting I did for a calendar. Generally, however, when an oil paint effect is sought, gouache is used to simulate the effect (see Chapter Seven).

Poster Paints

Poster paints are brilliant, opaque, nonbleeding paints. They are free-flowing because the pigments used are finely ground. Poster paints are also nonfugitive and dry to a flat matte finish that is very durable.

It is suggested they be used as prescribed, for posters and similar large flat jobs. They are not recommended for cards.

Higgins and Pelikan Colored Inks

Both Higgins and Pelikan colored inks are good, waterproof inks, specifically formulated for use with artists' and technical fountain pens, as well as air brushes. Both can be thinned with water

Figure 3-10
We're doing about the same as last year. And you?
(inside message), by Barbara and Jim Dale. This clever cartoon uses an ink drawing over a dropped-in pattern. Courtesy Recycled Paper Products, Inc.

for transparent washes or used full strength for line work. They come in one-ounce glass bottles with stoppers. There are eighteen colors. Black is available in eight-ounce and one-quart bottles as well.

Higgins F-100 Ink and Pelikan T Drawing Ink

Higgins F-100 ink and Pelikan T drawing ink are special black matte inks developed for use on drafting film. They do not peel or crack, and both reproduce very well. They are also acid-free and will not damage film surfaces. Both come in either one-ounce glass bottles or eight-ounce plastic bottles. The Higgins also comes in a 23 ml squeeze bottle.

Colored Markers

There are several contributors in colored markers with essentially the same characteristics. Most brands are of good quality with even flow until the supply begins to run dry. Markers will never rival gouache in card designing because they are less manipulative and offer a smaller range of effects. They are, however, quick, bright and fun to work with on occasion. I do know some designers who have adapted markers into their business on a larger scale.

Ad Markers

This is a fine-grade marker, available in two hundred colors. Adaptors (optional tips) can be purchased by the dozen. These come in four basic shapes: fine line, bullet-shaped, wedge-shaped, and brush-shaped. There are eight different sets to choose from.

Eberhard-Faber Design Art Markers

Eberhard-Faber Design Art Markers are narrow-bodied metal tubes and are suitable for layouts and fine arts. Three nibs are available: blunt, bullet, and fine line. There are ninety-six colors with the blunt nibs and forty-eight colors for each of the other tips. Eighteen different sets are offered.

Magic Markers

An assortment of magic markers in over 200 colors are sold. They are wide-bodied tubes and come with either a broad tip (about 150 colors) or a fine tip (about 50 colors).

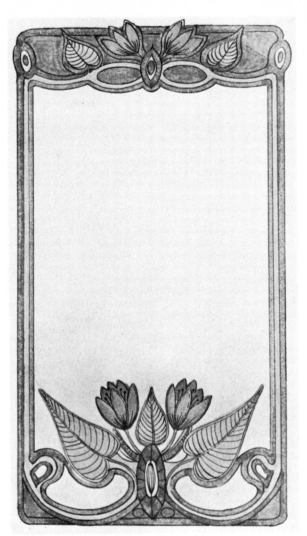

Figure 3-11
Water-based markers were used to paint in this border, gouache was used in the central areas, in this card by Ron Lister. Used by permission of Norcross-Rust Craft Divisions of Windsor Communications Group, Inc.

Stabilayout Pen Markers

Stabilayout pen markers are water-based markers that come in two series. The Series 68 has a slightly broader tip than the Series 38 layout marker. The Series 38 has a chisel-type tip, and is flat shaped to prevent rolling. The Series 68 pens are long and thin like a typical writing pen. Both series are available in fifty colors. They are great for detail work.

Pentel Fine Point Pen Markers

Pentel Fine Point pen markers are good-quality, water-based markers. They have a fine point for good control and use nontoxic ink that dries quickly. There are thirty-six nonbleed colors available.

Figure 3-12
In this card, by Sid Stromsdorfer, colored pencils were effectively used to add texture and interest to the design. Copyright by and courtesy of Renaissance Greeting Cards, Springvale, Maine.

Colored Pencils

Few cards use colored pencils as a predominant medium, but their use in spot work such as details, borders, scrollwork, touch-ups, and the like can be quite valuable. Here is an overview of some of the best wax-based and water-based brands.

Eagle Verithin and Prismacolor Pencils

Prismacolor pencils have been in use for a long time now. They are large-diameter pencils with soft leads that produce brilliant colors. The colors are waterproof and light-resistant, which makes them useful in card designing. There is one drawback regarding Prismacolor Pencils—their softness. Because the leads are both large and soft, I find them difficult to use in tight spots, especially where a sharp line is required. I prefer to use the Eagle Verithin pencils instead. Verithins are similar to Prismacolors except they are hexagonal instead of round and offer a stronger, thinner lead. The leads can be sharpened to a fine point for crisp line work or used more bluntly like the Prismacolors. Verithins are also less granular in appearance because of the harder lead.

34

There are forty Verithin and sixty Prisma-color pencils to choose from. They can be purchased in sets or singly.

Mongol Colored Pencils

Mongols are watercolor-based pencils. They are fairly large and round in shape and have a medium-hard lead. Because they are water-based, they will bleed when wet. In fact, if mixed with water, they break down like watercolor paints. This offers a wide variety of effects, and I have come to appreciate their many uses over the years. Sets come with twelve, twenty-four, and thirty-six colors.

Dixon Customer Color Pencils

Dixon Customer color pencils are thick-leaded pencils and are very soft. They produce a smooth, flowing line which is easily controllable. Sets include twelve and twenty-four colors each.

Pastels

I have been working with pastels for many years, mostly in a fine arts capacity. Only on occasion have I used them in card designing, but currently I am trying to sell some of my fine art

pastels to card publishers. They photograph well and offer many effects not possible with watercolors.

I recommend using soft pastels for blending into watercolors or for softening back watercolors that are too intense. Harder pastels and pastel pencils are better suited for drawing lines and detail work.

Of the various brands of soft pastels, I prefer Rembrandt's, made by Talens of Holland. They can be found easily and come separately or in sets of up to 180. Other good brands include Grumbacker in the United States and George Rowney in England.

Note: Oil pastels are oil-based. They do not act or react like soft pastels and are generally hard to control. I do not advise not using them in card designing.

MISCELLANEOUS MATERIALS

Technical Pens

Technical pens are designed to give even, free-flowing ink lines. They are good for use on acetates and drafting films, but are seldom used directly on cards. Line widths vary from 0.13 mm up to 2.0 mm, and there are several

Figure 3-13
Soft pastels were used by Ron Lister in this Valentine's Day card. Used by permission of Norcross-Rust Craft divisions of Windsor Communications Group, Inc.

Figure 3-14
Marion Moore makes good use of a technical pen to achieve a constant and uniform line in this card.
Courtesy of the artist, Brookline, Mass.

good brands to choose from including Faber Castell, Staedtler-Mars, Koh-I-Noor, and Dr. Martin's.

Hunt Artist Pens

Hunt offers the most recognized name in artist nibs and penholders. There are currently fourteen different nibs being sold. The 99 drawing nib has an extra-fine point for drafting and drawing. The 100 Artist nib is widely used for general designing, and the 102 Crow Quill is an excellent super-fine point used for fine-line work.

Drawing Pencils

Standard drawing pencils are relatively equal in range and quality. I have used Eagle Turquoise and Faber Castell (German) brands for years now, but other brands like Venus or Koh-I-Noor (black lead) are quite serviceable as well.

Drawing pencils are primarily used for thumbnail, rough, and finished sketches, as well as for transferring finished sketches onto the illustration board. Occasionally, they are used in finished designs.

Drawing pencils are classified by hardness of the lead tips. The softest leads are marked 6B and offer the darkest lines. The leads get progressively harder as the numbers go down from 6B to B. Pencils with a medium degree of hardness are numbered B, HB, and H, with H being the hardest of these. The numbering then goes back up from H to 9H, with 9H being the hardest and lightest pencil available. The soft B pencils are generally well-suited for rough sketches, while the H pencils are used more for finishing sketches and for transferring drawings onto the board.

Mechanical Pencils

Mechanical pencils, sometimes called *lead holders*, are serviceable for both sketching and transferring drawings. There are several models and brands to choose from. All use leads sold usually by the dozen. The leads come mostly in H and B hardnesses. Colored leads are available as well.

Mechanical Pencil Sharpeners (Lead Pointers)

There are quite a few sharpeners to choose from. Some are the small pocket variety that use blades to shave the leads. Other types include larger hand-held or clamp-on sharpeners. These use either replaceable blades or rough pads to sand down the leads. Top brands include Gedess (hand-held), Berol 17 (table model), Castell 42 (hand-held), and Koh-I-Noor (clamp).

Electric Pencil Sharpeners

A good pencil sharpener is a necessity. Whether it is electric is up to you, but the electric models are the quickest and easiest to use. Most have a sliding tray for easy cleaning and accept any size pencil.

Hand-Turned Pencil Sharpeners

Purchase a pencil sharpener that accepts a full range of pencil sizes. Some wide-bodied colored pencils may not fit into a single-hole sharpener.

Small models are hand-held. Larger ones either screw into the tabletop or use a suction cup base. I have used a suction-cup base sharpener for years. It has the advantage of being easily moved about.

Kneaded Erasers

I am certain most artists use a variety of erasers for different tasks. For soft jobs, kneaded erasers are quite useful. Besides erasing, they are capable of picking up chalk, pastel, charcoal, and graphite from the board surface. Also, they do not break up while being used, so fragments do not get in the way. Perhaps their biggest selling point is their flexibility. Kneaded erasers are soft and will not scratch the board, and being flexible, they can be shaped in your hand to reach small, hard-to-get-at areas. Top brands include Eberhard-Faber and Conte. Conte also sells an extra-soft kneaded eraser.

Typewriter Erasers

Of the more conventional erasers, typewriter erasers are very useful to the artist. They are hard and abrasive, so their use on delicate papers should be avoided; but they are well-suited for tough jobs, like removing paint or softening colors.

Electric Erasers

Sometimes my students think I am humoring them when I explain that electric erasers are part of the job, but it is true. Most card designers I know use them. I use a common cord-type model with a small motor at the top. There are also cordless and rechargeable battery-operated styles as well.

All models use long, refillable eraser strips, seven inches in length and a quarter-inch in diameter. These strips come in a variety of soft to hard surfaces. Between the different types, almost any surface can be safely worked on.

Rulers

The best rulers are metal or aluminum with a rubber or soft material backing which prevents slipping and keeps ink from bleeding underneath the edge. I prefer rulers with both metric and inch calibrations on one side.

Note: If your ruler or ruling edge does not have a backing, try taping a couple of dimes or thin strips of cardboard to the reverse side. This will raise the surface and prevent ink from bleeding underneath and being dragged across the paper surface.

Templates

Templates are transparent plastic aids, from simple geometric shapes such as circles, ovals, and the like to more complex and specific shapes used in lettering, architecture, and engineering. I find sets of small circles, ovals, and ellipses are

Figure 3-15
Ron Lister uses a tracing to show how different templates and a compass can be employed. The actual card was later done in gold leaf on a precepted background.

especially useful. It is difficult to use a compass for very small circles or a French curve for very small ovals and ellipses.

Curves (French Curves)

French curves are transparent templates that provide a variety of irregular curves. The best ones are made of acrylic plastic and will not yellow or break. French curves can be bought individually or in any number of sets. Flexible curves made of vinyl plastic are also available. These allow adjustments to be made at will.

Triangles

Of the various angles sold, a good 90° triangle is most helpful. I still use one to start every job. They are also useful for borders and for double-checking other angles.

Magnifiers and Reducers

Since most cards are done to scale, a magnifying glass is very useful. I use a small mounted model, but hand-held magnifiers are preferred by many. If you should find yourself doing cards scaled up in size, then a reducing glass may be necessary. It can be difficult to visualize a smaller format when working large. Reducers show the card as it will look when scaled down to size.

Compasses

I suggest buying a good compass as it will not only last longer, but will likely be more accurate as well. Good compasses have interchangeable parts: ruling pens, extension arms, cutting blades, and divider points.

Compass sets are quite expensive these days. It might be worth keeping an eye out for old sets being sold at antique shops or flea markets. This is one area where the old products are generally better-made than the new ones.

Note: Besides my good compass set, I also own a couple of 98¢ school compasses. These hold regular size pencils and are good when using colored pencils. (Regular compasses hold lead points, not whole pencils.)

X-Acto Knives

X-Acto knives are precision tools for controlled cutting. A variety of blades can be fitted for different tasks. I use a straight blade for cutting mats and straight edges, and a curved blade for more complex cutting. Swivel blades are also available for doing curves.

Mat Knives

Mat knives carry heavier cutting blades. They are adjustable, and the blades are replaceable. They are good for cutting heavy mats, packaging materials, and even boards.

Paper Cutters

It is worth having a paper cutter if you plan to be a commercial designer. Some materials (tissue paper, tracing paper, and the like) are difficult to cut with an X-Acto knife, and illustration board is hard to cut even with a heavy mat knife.

Paper cutters come in standard sizes. I have a 15″ cutter and find I could use a bigger one at times, but prices will undoubtedly help you decide on which size to buy. Pressed wood and plastic paper cutters have largely replaced the older wood-type paper cutters.

Tapes and Adhesives

Conventional cellophane tape is serviceable for borders and most jobs. Masking tapes are good for packaging and heavier jobs.

As for adhesives, rubber cement is a good product for temporary bonding of surfaces. Double-sticking the surfaces creates a longer bond, but rubber cement yellows with age. It also seeps through paper and will eventually dis-color. The best aspect of rubber cement is that it can be applied evenly and smoothly. Pastes and glues tend to be spotty and uneven.

Furniture

A good drawing table, taboret, flat filing cabinet, light table, and so on are all items that are bought as the need arises. It is possible to do without any of the above, but not much fun. A good drawing table is nearly a necessity. Besides being very sturdy, they are adjustable and can be altered to fit your own size comfortably.

Lamps

The most important item is a good drawing lamp. I use a clamping type that takes two fluorescent tubes. I use one cool and one warm tube together for balance, though two cool tubes are equally serviceable.

Note: It is important to use fluorescent lighting if you cannot use natural sunlight. Regular house bulbs are very warm and are not suitable for seeing and reproducing good, accurate colors.

Chairs and Stools

Anyone who has worked for any length of time without a good chair or stool knows the value of having one. I prefer a swivel chair with arms, but good ones are expensive. I bought mine at a used office furniture store. It is in mint condition and cost approximately one-quarter of what a new one would.

Chapter Four

The Basic Card

`A Birthday Thought

Figure 4-1
Ron Lister demonstrating step four.
Courtesy of Red Farm Studio.

Over the next two chapters, we will look at the basic steps involved in designing a greeting card and at some of the "hidden" rules which govern layout and design.

In terms of time and energy, painting a card is not terribly difficult. The majority of cards are painted to exact size, approximately 5″ × 7″. This is a small format to begin with, and painting with watercolors helps to speed up the process even further. In fact, if there is no immediate deadline, painting a card is quite relaxing. Most take only a day or two to complete, and simple designs may take only a matter of a few hours. However, I do know artists who work very slowly and methodically, taking upwards of a week or two to complete a job. Working quickly is not a prerequisite, but it can help.

If there were no other considerations, the

majority of us could paint several cards a week. The reality is, of course, somewhat different.

I believe we spend more time preparing to paint a card than we do in actually painting it. First, we must go out and get the assignment, and second, we have to collect the necessary reference materials for laying out the design. Only then can the card be painted.

Contrary to what many people outside the card field believe, cards are not created solely within our imaginations. A good imagination may be a useful commodity, but it is good reference and keen observation that keep us going. Even cartooning, which is generally thought of as a purely creative endeavor, relies heavily on close observation of people and animals, as well as other cartoon styles and techniques.

The greeting card field is a highly skilled one, and within it, nearly all artists are required to specialize by concentrating their efforts on a limited number of subjects or areas. Collecting reference for cards is itself a specialized endeavor. The majority of materials can be easily found in published form: books, magazines, other cards, and so on; but often we are required to seek out reference in more unusual places.

The longer we work as commercial artists,

the larger our private stockpiles of reference become. This happens out of necessity. It is surprising how much good reference material can help. It is also surprising how much of it is needed. I strongly suggest starting now on your own reference library. Remember, a good library can save valuable time and energy. It is very frustrating to have to stop work on a card until you can locate a needed piece of reference. It can break up your continuity and concentration.

COLLECTING REFERENCE

Catalogs

For those of us who live in urban areas, collecting reference is not terribly difficult. Between libraries and newsstands, a wide variety of materials are readily available. Buying magazines and books can be expensive, however, and library books must be returned. With this in mind, many of us are constantly searching for inexpensive ways to collect materials. Old magazines and books are always being thrown out. Start asking your friends and relatives to save them for you. Send away for free catalogs and brochures when possible. Large department stores

Figure 4-2
Because the majority of cards are painted out of season, it is necessary to take reference pictures year round. This photo of Magnolias by Ron Lister is just one of hundreds the author keeps on file.

give catalogs away once or twice a year. Find out when. Also, if you buy something once from a small mail order catalog, you will likely start receiving a whole range of other catalogs. It appears to be easy to get on such a mailing list.

For floral and landscape artists, there are several good seed company catalogs. Wayside Gardens in Hodges, South Carolina, publishes a beautiful catalog of flowers and shrubs twice per year. Better yet, why not buy some seeds and start growing your own reference? There is no substitute for the real thing.

For scenic references, several airlines offer exceptional travel catalogs. Champion Papers also publishes a beautiful series called "Imagination," which features different peoples and places from around the world.

The list is too long to describe adequately. There are countless other catalogs available for the asking. Many companies have sales catalogs or brochures that can be purchased or acquired for free. Of special interest for us are greeting card sales catalogs. Whenever I am in contact with a card publisher for the first time, I ask if a catalog or any promotional materials are available. Most companies will send one out for free. A few charge a nominal fee, but you must ask.

Magazines

Each week, hundreds of magazines are published worldwide. There is a magazine for almost every conceivable interest. Yet, while subscribing to a variety of publications is fun, I find it unnecessary. Living in Boston, I find a large variety of national and international magazines are available. I prefer to pay periodic visits to the best news shops and buy specific issues off the rack as needed.

Another way to save money is to take advantage of public libraries. Although few libraries carry a wide variety of specialized magazines, they usually stock a few. Between college and public libraries, almost any magazine can be found. If your library or branch does not offer what you need, ask the librarians which other libraries do carry the magazine you need. They will be glad to tell you.

The majority of magazines found in libraries cannot be signed out, so there are two basic options: bring your work into the library or photocopy what you need. It is worth the effort.

Figure 4-3
Canadian Geese. The author used several pieces of reference to create this scene.

Books

For our purpose, there are two categories of books I would like to mention. First are those books termed *publishers' overstocks*. These are generally large-format, pictorial books, printed in large editions. There is often one printing, and the prices are kept low. Copies which do not sell within a fairly short time are then further reduced for final clearance. In order to reach the broadest public market, the books cover general topics and are full of color. The Color Nature Library, printed by Crescent Books, a division of Crown Publishers, is an inexpensively-priced series on nature. There are more than fifteen books, covering birds, animals, and flowers. Other publishers offer essentially the same range of topics and interests.

If you cannot find a good bookstore that sells books at reduced prices, it is possible to obtain many of them through book clubs, especially clearinghouse-type book clubs.

A second type of reference book is that sold expressly for graphic artists. The largest such series is the Dover Pictorial Archive Series, printed by Dover Publications, Inc., of New York. This edition includes more than thirty mostly large-format books printed in black and white. They are collections of visual design motifs, ranging from early advertising illustrations to art nouveau and art deco designs. Topics include symbols, signs, lettering, textile and carpet designs, and ornamental patterns from around the world.

There are quite a few other publications offering visual motifs. I have a couple of old books on early advertising art (nineteenth century) and several more on twentieth-century commercial and fine arts. I obtained most of these from used-book stores at a good saving.

Miscellaneous Reference Sources

As a rule, the better the reference, the easier it is to interpret from it what we need. According to this axiom, photographs are generally preferred over illustrations, color photographs over black and white, and so on; but life provides the only true, time-tested reference. The reason is simple. A photograph can provide only one angle with one light source at a time. If the angle, point of view, and distance shown in the photograph are precisely what is needed, all is well, but normally, things must be altered to fit. Drawing from nature is the only way I know to take full advantage of a subject. Whenever I can, I sketch from life. I also collect as many natural objects as possible: pine cones, dried flowers, and the like. I even keep a set of artificial (paper and silk) flowers around in order to be able to draw exact angles or to put a precise light source on them.

Still, opportunities to sketch and collect from nature are limited, and I find my camera has become my best tool. Like most artists, I use a 35 mm single reflex camera. Optional lenses (close-up, wide field, telephoto) provide any extra help I need to capture the subject in the best way. Instant cameras generally do not take great pictures, but they do offer the artist an immediate result to compare and analyze. For years I have been taking reference photographs for my library. I try to keep in mind that cards are done out of season. So I must shoot my winter scenes for the next summer's use. The only way to do this is to take pictures expressly for reference, to be conscious of what you might need in the coming months. This applies to collecting greeting cards as well. In the summer months, when painting Santa Claus, it is impossible to find him on the card racks. Again, I suggest starting a collection now.

Organization of Reference

Collecting reference is time-consuming, expensive, and exhausting. Not being able to find the right piece of reference when needed can be the final blow to an artist. To the commercial designer, time is money, and good organization will save time. Whether you like to be systematic or not, maintaining a system is imperative.

There are various ways to store materials; folding envelopes, expanding folders, leaf folders, drawers, and shelves can all help. It is not important how reference materials are kept, as long as they are kept safe from damage and are well-organized for quick and easy use. Even old shoe boxes can be suitable. My own system has evolved over the years. I use a combination of expanding folders and large wooden bins. Each folder contains a subject which is further divided by single white dividers. All the folders are filed in the wooden bins. Approximately once each week, I take an hour or two out for refiling and cleaning up. This careful organization is important to me. When reference materials are messy, other problems usually ensue.

PAINTING A CARD: A DEMONSTRATION

This demonstration is to show how a basic greeting card is designed and painted. It also offers a chance to put to use some of the art reference materials discussed previously.

Figure 4-4
By Ron Lister. This photo shows the rough sketch used
for the final design of Figure 4-5.

Figure 4-5
In the finished card, the foreground areas were altered
considerably from the previous sketch (Figure 4-4). Otherwise, the scene remains quite similar.

Getting the assignment and receiving the *specifications* (a specific work order) will be discussed in Chapter Eleven (see "Creation of a Card"). At this point, it is assumed subject, format, and specific references have been chosen, and painting the card is all that remains to be done.

Note: The card I chose for this demonstration is a simple one. It involves no special overlays nor does it require any special techniques.

Initial Sketches

Several *thumbnail* sketches may be required at first. These are very small pencil drawings done on tracing paper. Thumbnail sketches may vary somewhat but are usually rough or crude designs that enable us to visualize all the elements of the card quickly. My thumbnails are approximately 2″ × 3″ in size, but may be larger if the card is more complicated. These rough sketches are sometimes done on drawing paper or layout

paper, but tracing paper is best. I generally use a 2B or 3B drawing pencil at this stage.

How many thumbnail sketches are needed depends on how much of the initial layout has been thought out in advance. However, by doing several sketches, it is likely one will appear superior to the others. It may turn out to be the first sketch drawn, but often it is one of the latter ones that best fits the specifications. For this reason, I recommend doing more than one quick sketch, even if you are satisfied with your initial attempt.

One way to design different layouts is to take the separate components of the card individually. In this demonstration, those components include several birds, a wagon wheel, a tree, and some flowers. In the original sketches, different arrangements of these components could be tried out, as well as more specific choices, such as what type of tree, flowers, or birds to use. At this stage, these separate elements are composed in different ways. The best angle, perspective, light source, and sizes of each element are chosen. Once this

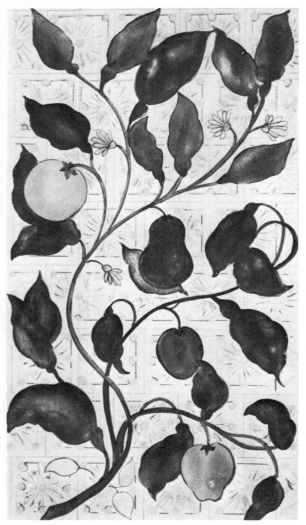

Figure 4-6
A colored rough painted by the author.

is accomplished, the finished drawing can be started.

Note: All companies, when assigning work, ask that drawings or painted sketches be submitted for approval before a finished card is painted. These unfinished designs, whether pencil sketches or small painted sketches, are all termed *roughs*. For more on roughs, see Chapter Ten.

Intermediate Drawings

Depending on how involved the card is, several intermediate drawings may be needed before a finished drawing, ready for transfer, can be done.

Generally, the thumbnail sketch is enlarged to full size, in this case, $4^3/4'' \times 6^3/4''$. On tracing paper, a fairly rough drawing is made from the original thumbnail sketch. If the design is simple, this can be done by *eyeballing* the smaller sketch. Eyeballing means to visually estimate the larger sketch from the smaller one. If the design is complicated, then a *Camera Lucinda* can be used to enlarge the thumbnail. If you cannot get to a Camera Lucinda (Lucy Camera), the design can still be enlarged and transferred by *graphing* the two sketches. This refers to making a grid over both sketches of equal proportion and then transposing from the smaller grid to the larger grid. Photo-realist painters and illustrators often use this method.

Once the design has been enlarged, it can then be refined by placing successive pieces of tracing paper over each other while tightening up the drawing and making detailed changes. Again, this process varies from job to job and from artist to artist. The experienced artist may skip some or all of these stages to arrive at a finished drawing. I have known some artists who start by drawing directly on the illustration board.

The Finished Drawing (Figure 4-8)

After these initial stages have been completed, I then have a fairly tight drawing I can use for transferring. The next step is to delete any unnecessary elements from the drawing before transferring it to the illustration board.

Transferring the Drawing

Step One

Step one begins by taking a 90° triangle (or T-square), along with a ruling edge, and measuring out the correct dimensions of the card. This step normally includes the *bleed*. The bleed is a predetermined area around the perimeter of the design. It is a safety precaution which allows for any minor problems that may arise later during the printing and folding of the card (see Figure 4-7). A typical bleed might include a $^1/16''$ area along the folding edge of the card and a $^1/8''$ or $^3/16''$ area around the rest of the design. In this assignment, a $^1/16''$ bleed is used on the folding edge and a $^1/8''$ bleed on the other edges. The actual card dimensions are $4^1/2'' \times 6^3/4''$, but with

Figure 4-7

This is an entire design, by Ron Lister, complete with corner marks, bleed marks, and company identification numbers. This card was apparently a two dollar boxed set and was sold in the U.K., Canada, and the U.S. Used by permission of Norcross-Rust Craft divisions of Windsor Communications Group, Inc.

the bleeds added, the painted dimensions are now $4^{15}/_{16}''$ ($^1/_{16}'' + ^1/_8''$) $\times$ $7''$ ($^1/_8'' + ^1/_8''$).

The outer perimeters along the bleeds are now lined with transparent tape to mask off the area around the edge of the card. This keeps the illustration looking neat and professional and also allows us to see the edge of the design more clearly as we work. *Note*: Some designers keep ready-made mats nearby and constantly use them to help visualize the card as it progresses.

The illustration board is then trimmed in the paper cutter, leaving a two-inch border on which the publisher will place registration and

identification numbers. Figure 4-7 shows an actual card complete with all these identification marks.

Once the card is taped and the measurements double-checked for error, the tracing with the finished drawing is placed over the board and taped lightly along the top. A sheet of *graphite transfer paper* is then slipped between the two surfaces, and a hard (5H) pencil is used to draw over the tracing. Moderate pressure is used in order to fully transfer the drawing to the board beneath the transfer paper.

When this is done, the tracing and transfer

Figure 4-8
Demonstration of step one
showing the final tracing.

papers are removed, and a kneaded eraser is
used to pick up the excess graphite from the
new drawing. I like to make the drawing as light
as possible, so it will not show through the final
painting.

Step Two

Figure 4-9 shows the final transfer on the board,
with some of the initial wash tones already added.

At this stage, a loose, transparent wash of
ochre and browns is placed around the tree and
in the foreground areas. By keeping the board
wet during this part, I am able to vignette (fade
off) the wash in the title area. A smooth tran-
sition is necessary.

Here, a decision is made concerning the
flowers in the foreground. Liquid mask is not
used to block out those areas where the white

Figure 4-9
Demonstration of step two with
the transferred drawing and
some initial wash tones.

flowers are needed. Instead, I carefully paint in the white areas over the wash undercoat. This is done for two reasons: first, to let a little of the color beneath show through the flowers' petals, and second, to allow myself the opportunity to "hit" in the flower petals with short, quick brush strokes. Masking out each petal would look tight and possibly contrived as well.

Note: Watercolors, not designers, gouache,

is used on this card. Red Farm Studio likes to keep its look fresh and light. Opaque colors are not generally encouraged, nor are hard outlines around objects.

Step Three

Slowly, the wash tones are built up (Figure 4-10). The birch tree is painted in with light washes of browns, blue-grays, and ochres. The wagon wheel

Figure 4-10
Demonstration of step three.

is developed with red-brown tones, light siennas, and yellow ochres, along with Payne's Gray in the shadows.

The foreground is then filled in around and partly over the white flowers. Darker tones are added with olive green and grays, but without letting those undertones become muddy or dirty.

In some ways, working with transparent wash tones is more difficult than working with opaque colors. Correct values must be maintained throughout the work because reworking areas cannot be done with paint, although minimal erasing is possible.

Finally, the birds are begun with cerulean blue, sienna red, and a touch of yellow ochre to add warmth.

Step Four

The last phase of the card includes tightening up the rendering of the wheel and adding final values to it. A brown Verithin colored pencil is used to tighten up the rim of the wheel and the spokes (Figure 4-1 and Plate 12).

Next, the flowers are painted in with non-bleed white. Then, a little touch of blue and gray is added to the shadowed portions of the petals, while a touch of warm yellow is added to the sun portions of the flowers. The leaves and surrounding areas are finalized, and details added throughout. In some areas, a kneaded eraser is used to soften back some color.

Throughout the design, the browns are predominant. However, the small touches of blue and red in the birds remain quite important because they offer the only relief from those browns. In this way and by their placement within the composition, the birds become the central theme of the design along with the wagon wheel. To help with this connection of themes, the birds are shown directly reacting to the wheel by either gazing at it or by flying down toward it.

The last touch is a light wash of warm yellow and ochre throughout parts of the design. A warm-brown border is then cut from paper stock and placed over the design. This allows the publisher to change the color of the border or discard it if desired. Most cards do not need borders, but in this case, I feel that the design is a bit on the light side and a darker border will help to frame the picture and contain it. It also serves as a sort of window in this particular design.

CONCLUSION

Even though this card was not a complicated drawing nor a difficult painting, there was still a good deal to consider.

Any card requires that not only must you like it, but the publisher must like it too. To this end, all elements of the design must be carefully planned. Remember, any design is only as good as its weakest component, and a publisher is going to put hundreds or thousands of dollars into that design by the end. I have one recommendation concerning this. If all blemishes and mistakes cannot be entirely removed from the finished design without showing, it is better to do the whole card over again. Remember, if you can find it, so will the art director.

Figure 4-11
By Marge Pendleton. Courtesy of Red Farm Studio.

Note: This demonstration was accomplished by retracing my steps in designing and creating a card that was previously sold. Any slight deviations between the initial steps and the final card should be disregarded as nonessential.

Profile:
Red Farm Studio

My association with Red Farm Studio goes back to 1975. During this time, I have been greatly impressed by the consistent quality of Red Farm products. For this profile, I asked Mr. J. Parker Scott, the President, if he would outline for me how Red Farm cards are printed with such care and control, as well as a little of the company's history. I thank him for the information provided.

Ellen Nelson, an artist from Reading, Massachusetts, founded Red Farm Studio in 1947. She had begun, like so many others, by hand-painting a few Christmas cards for her friends. With encouragement, she started a business. The business name refers to the Nelson home, a red house on a large tract of land where ponies were raised. Mrs. Nelson ran the company for the next ten years, but in 1958, the Scott family, who owned Cardinal Greetings, Inc., purchased Red Farm and merged the two small companies. In 1958, the company sold cards only in New England. Today, their sales territories cover all fifty states, and include a large catalog of cards and related paper products, some of which are still designed by Mrs. Nelson.

Red Farm Studio is a family-oriented company. Their cards are conservative and traditional. The entire line, which is painted by a small in-house staff and selected freelance artists, maintains the Red Farm image. Once the cards are painted, the company goes to great lengths to ensure the final product will meet the expected standard.

The bulk of Red Farm's color separations are done by a company in Brussels, Belgium, with all the latest equipment that still employs craftspeople who take the time and effort to hand etch the films. Each piece of art is handled individually. Some are separated by camera, others by laser scanner, while the rest are done on a klischograph. By using different processes, each card is color-separated to bring out the necessary subtle tones and vignettes that are associated with Red Farm cards.

For many years, Red Farm traveled equally far to have its printing done. Now, however, the color lithography is done by United Printing Co. of Warwick, Rhode Island, which uses the latest technology and equipment.

In the final analysis, Red Farm Studio has developed slowly and carefully. It has maintained a quality-over-quantity system that has produced simple, refined, and subtle cards for many years. Red Farm is still a relatively small company, but one with high-quality products due to high standards and control.

Chapter Five

No Belly Buttons, Please

Figure 5-1 *Steve* by Nancy Kellerman.
Courtesy of the artist, Boston, Mass.

MORE BASICS OF LAYOUT AND DESIGN: WORKING ON SPECS

There are numerous dos and don'ts in the greeting card field. Some of the things we should or should not do are dictated to us by the companies we work for, but in this business there are many "hidden" rules which do not appear on spec sheets (written directions).

Most designers develop a method for solving the basic problems of layout and design, to the point where it becomes second nature. Like any new technique, all considerations must be kept on a conscious level until they actually do become second nature. Unfortunately, it is very difficult to learn even the basic ins and outs of the card field without actually being in the field itself. Several artists interviewed for this book stressed this fact and recommended working as a full-time card designer, if at all possible.

Each company has its own look and a set of regulations to ensure that look is realized. On the surface, big companies may appear to have a variety of looks and styles, but in fact, most companies can be identified fairly easily by direct comparison.

Each company helps its freelance artists by sending out a list of specs. Periodically, a *general specification sheet* may be sent out. This describes what the company is presently looking for. Such a list might include the number of designs needed to fill a certain line. Using the Christmas line as an example, a general specification sheet might categorize the number of cards needed according to subject or theme—that is, three Santas, four manger scenes, two fireplace settings, and the like. New card sizes, bleeds, and other technical information would also be included. Beyond that, it is up to the artist to submit sketches for approval. This process is termed *working on speculation*. Doing work without the benefit of even general specifications is termed *stockpiling*. In stockpiling, the artist first finishes a number of designs and then tries to sell them collectively or individually to a company.

Note: When a publisher first announces that it is beginning a new line, it is a good time to submit cards you have stockpiled. Many card designers try to do some work in this fashion during the summer months when things are slow. Later, when the new fall and winter lines begin, they will have some cards (or rough sketches) ready to go.

When planning to submit work on speculation, either rough or finished designs, be sure you know exactly what your publisher is looking for. I always ask for either samples or company sales catalogs. Even if I know the company well, I still ask periodically for new samples. This has a bearing on what I will submit. If I see in last year's catalog a design featuring cardinals on a branch near a birdhouse, then I will know not to submit a design too similar to that. However, if such a card appeared in a catalog five years earlier and has not appeared since, then I may try a similar motif on purpose. The aim is well-defined; we want to submit work that fits in with the company's look, so it must be similar in cer-

tain respects to the company's previously published cards. On the other hand, cards that are too similar will not be useful. Card companies are always searching for something new but similar to their established look.

In freelancing and in full-time employment, there is a second fundamental method of assigning work, in which the art director assigns very detailed and specific job orders termed *specifications*. Sometimes, this is a general list of dos and don'ts as discussed. Other times, the work assignment is itemized very explicitly, leaving the artist only to fill the requirements. For more on these subjects, see Chapters Ten and Eleven.

BASIC LAYOUTS

In advertising and commercial art, there are several basic layouts to be considered. These are essentially broad categories in which different

Figure 5-2
Ron Lister used panels to group the subjects and the caption together. In this way, each element can be handled separately and still be tied to the main theme. Courtesy of Red Farm Studio.

Figure 5-3
By Anatoly Dverin. In a *path* type layout, the viewers eye is lead through the design and towards the upper right hand corner where the title or captions will go. Used by permission of Norcross-Rust Craft Divisions of Windsor Communications Group, Inc.

types of layouts can be labeled. The quickest, easiest, and least expensive layouts are *grid* types, used primarily in advertising. Department stores, drugstores, and food markets often print up sales flyers using a grid system. The grid consists of vertical and horizontal lines that simply block the page into a variety of rectangles or squares. In cards, grid-type formats are seldom used. The closest format is the *panel* type (see Figure 5-2). In this card, the different elements have been placed within the various panels, with one panel left for the caption. The panels are simple, and the variations between them are minimal but necessary. The caption or title in this card lies in the middle right panel on the cut or open side of the card. The only other possibility would have been to combine the two smaller top panels and include the caption there. *Note*: Captions seldom, if ever, rest against the folding side of a card.

The two most favored layouts in cards are the *path* and *group* types. In the path format (see Figure 5-3), the eye is led from point to point within the design, with the most important point being the caption area. Again, the upper-right

portion of the card is most often used for the title or caption, so the various elements of the card should lead the eye towards that area. In Figure 5-3, the hood ornament and the two cars lead the eye naturally in that direction.

A variation of the path layout is the *border* format. Figure 5-5 shows a Christmas border in which the birds and foliage completely encircle the perimeters of the card. The middle area is then left open for the verse. Border-type cards come in many varieties: V-shaped borders, L-shaped borders, and so on. The most important consideration is to leave enough room for the caption in the middle (or sometimes above). This means not allowing any of the visual elements to protrude too far out into the verse area. Sometimes, if we know the verse, we can plan the border to blend into it, but for the most part, we must guess how long it will be and leave ample room for it.

Finally, the *group* layout is the format most often employed. In this format, the visual elements are attached physically, making the outline of the group the most important aspect of the design. The outline is the first thing we see; within it, individual elements then become recognized. The caption is sometimes, though infrequently, a part of the main group. To accomplish this, a panel or note card may be drawn into the composition, with the caption appearing inside. By using calligraphy, the caption can be integrated into the group without the shelter of a panel or framed note card. Still, the standard visual concept is to include the caption in the negative space created by the more positive forms of the group. In Figure 5-4, and Color Plate 6, we see a still life design that uses kitchen objects to form two separate groups. Within the negative space created by these groups, the verse "Wishing You Birthday Joy" appears.

There are numerous examples of group layouts in this book. In fact, all the cards fall into one or more of these basic categories. There is a good deal of overlapping. A path layout may also be planned in a group format, and, as mentioned, a border layout is really a variation of the path layout.

How important is all of this? Certainly, a major portion of these concepts become second nature after awhile; but it is especially important for beginners to know how to vary their layouts and take advantage of these variations to create

Figure 5-4
By Nancy Kellerman. In a *group* layout, the outline becomes the most prominent element of the design. Here it is used to frame the caption. Courtesy of Red Farm Studio.

new designs, designs that use the same visual elements, motifs, and subjects. In this way, even the old pro has use for these layout concepts. After years of designing the same themes, we need all the help we can get.

Leaving Caption Room

There has been a trend over the past few years towards shorter captions. Some of the smaller publishers are producing cards without any caption or verse. Even the larger companies are doing it to some extent, with boxed Christmas cards being the primary example. Still, the vast majority of cards do have captions. Market research experts have proven that people tend to buy cards more because of the verse (sentiment) than the design. Good designs may help, but apparently the first thing consumers look for is an appropriate caption, something that addresses the occasion and sentiment fairly specifically. If

Mom wants to buy a birthday card for her son, she is likely to look first for a caption that fits the occasion. To many designers, this is a harsh reality. Over the years, one of the most often asked questions has been "Do you write those verses?" The answer is no. I have wondered at times why captions sell so well when many people do not seem to like them, but again, we must look to those who buy the majority of cards. Captions specify the occasion, and verses often say what the buyer is not able to say.

When freelancing, it is often impossible to find out what the caption is going to be. So we must allow ample room for it. The better we know the publisher, the more we can guess at this, but as a rule, when in doubt, leave a little extra room.

To summarize, when designing a card, it is imperative that the visual elements of the design

Figure 5-5
By Ron Lister. In a border type design, it is necessary to leave plenty of room for the verse. Elements that protrude into the central areas of the card can create a problem. Courtesy of Red Farm Studio.

lead the eye towards the caption or verse, never away from it. Most captions are at the top or top right-hand corner of the card. This is to ensure the sentiment can be read when the cards are placed in the store racks. For designers, this means we are expected to lead the eye towards the top or top right-hand corner of the card.

NO BELLY BUTTONS, PLEASE

Throughout this book, quite a few of the hidden rules of the card business can be found. Rules concerning layout and design often involve simple common sense. Leading the eye toward the cutting side of the card makes sense, as the inside verse is an important part of the overall concept. However, in this business, there are many truly hidden rules that apply to specific situations and subjects. "No belly buttons, please," refers to a comment made by Judy Mitchell while we were doing her profile (see Chapter Eight). It concerns an unwritten rule which applies to drawing teddy bears. Judy also mentioned several rules about drawing babies. All babies are born at six months of age. All babies have blue eyes. Even their curls are accounted for, and, of course, so are the colors. Blue is still for boys and pink for girls. The list is quite extensive and varies from company to company, and time effects changes as well. In the past, men could not have moustaches unless the theme was a nostalgic one. Hair could not touch the ears. Later, hair could cover just the top of the ear, then a bit more, and so on. Today, the rules have relaxed considerably, but they still exist. Because it is impossible to detail this further, it is best to make sure you understand what your publisher is looking for. Use the telephone if necessary. When in doubt, ask questions. It can save some big headaches.

Note: The rules concerning juvenile and figurative cards are still more stringently adhered to than most other card types. Have you ever tried to draw an ageless figure or neuter child? In greeting cards, this is required, primarily because companies are trying to reach as broad a consumer base as possible. Sex and age are seen as limitations.

USING POSITIVE
AND NEGATIVE SHAPES

Up until the 1970s, negative space was not a primary concern. Cards were filled with detail and ornamentation. Positive space dominated.

Figure 5-6
This striking design by Gordon Semmens makes good use of positive-negative relationships. Copyright by and courtesy of Renaissance Greeting Cards, Springvale, Maine.

Gradually, this changed. Figure 5-6 shows a handsome card designed for Renaissance. The giraffe has been placed in the very center of the composition. Usually, this is not a good idea, but here the artist has counterbalanced the design by making the background trees asymmetrical. Remember, symmetry in a composition can be boring. This card displays quite a range of contrast, which places a greater emphasis on both the positive (dark) and negative (white) shapes. This makes the blank negative areas almost as important as the positive shapes of the giraffe and trees.

Much of our understanding of the importance of negative space has been brought to us from the East. In the mid to late nineteenth century, many Japanese colored prints found their way to Europe and America. The Impressionist painters, especially Degas, Monet, and Pissarro, were strongly influenced by the Japanese use of two-dimensional space that created such strong positive-negative relationships.

Most of us are familiar with Impressionism. So I suggest looking directly at the eighteenth- and nineteenth-century Japanese printmakers. The greatest artists are Hiroshige, Kiyonaga, Harunoba, Shunsho, and Hokusai, whose thirty-six views of Mt. Fuji are renowned. I especially recommend looking at the works of Utamaro (see Figure 5-7). His colored wood blocks are among the greatest compositions of all time. Each element, area, and movement in an Utamaro print were designed with grace and dignity. Other than the great French painter J. B. Chardin, I can think of no other artist who equals Utamaro's wonderful sense of design.

Figure 5-7
This 18th century wood block print was done by Utamaro who was a master of composition. Each element in this print is carefully related to the overall concept of the work.

Figure 5-8
Love will find a way by Leo Sauer. Copyright by and courtesy of Renaissance Greeting Cards, Springvale, Maine.

Profile:
Renaissance Cards

Of the numerous small card publishers that began during the 1970s, perhaps none had a more inauspicious start than Renaissance. Yet Renaissance cards are currently selling very well, and their future looks bright. Their story began in 1975, when a small group of friends designed a silk-screened Christmas card for their friends. The card was a great success, and six pen and ink designs were made for the following Christmas season. A moderate fee was charged to cover printing costs, and this in turn provided funds for more designs to be printed. Going into 1977, there was still no formal organization. All those involved still held full-time jobs. However, one member of the group did begin visiting retail shops and selling directly to them. The following year, a prominent New England sales representative began to market Renaissance cards, and the business started to take off. By 1982, their catalog showed over one thousand designs. Today, there is a small full-time staff, a large number of freelance artists, and an ever-growing market for Renaissance designs.

Renaissance reflects the best of the contemporary market, though not the most radical. In fact, Ron Sellers, one of the original founders, states that his company is one of the more conservative of the new publishers. But he points out that the new market only comprises a small percent of the overall market and that the overall market is still considerably more conservative than Renaissance.

How do Renaissance designs differ from those of the larger market? First, they vary widely in subject, content, and treatment. Subjective colors, those which involve personal judgments (see Chapter Three), comprise a major portion of the line. Because Renaissance is willing to look at and purchase from a wide variety of freelance artists, their products reflect many personal touches provided by those artists. The general line is expressive, decorative, and tasteful.

Mr. Sellers informs me that the majority of the Renaissance lines are designed on a freelance basis and they are willing to review any art sent to them.

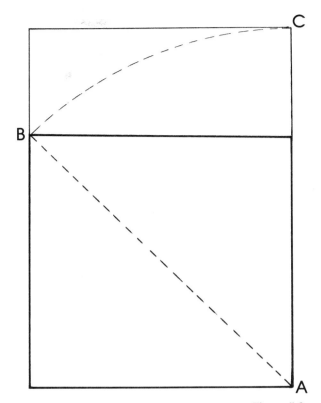

Figure 5-9

Card proportion. The 1:1.4 ratio is considered an ideal format. To make this proportion, connect a compass from point A to point B and follow to point C. Connect the outer edges by using a ninety-degree triangle.

CARD PROPORTION

In advertising and general design, there is a basic proportion (1 to 1.4) that is commonly accepted as the ideal format. This formula, with slight variations, can be seen in most commercial designs. Books, magazines, cards, and stationery have common proportions. The average card size of 5″ × 7″ closely resembles this 1 to 1.4 ratio. It is hard to argue that such dimensions are not pleasing to the eye, and when working with elongated card sizes, the 5″ × 7″ dimensions look even better. Elongated cards are somewhat common. They are used almost exclusively in studio lines (see Chapter Six), which are typically flat or two-dimensional. With studio cards, the gag line and the visual elements can be read vertically without much trouble. However, designing conventional cards with the same dimensions (roughly 4½″ × 8″) is a real problem.

It is difficult to fit the illusion of three dimensions comfortably into such a skinny format. Cars and ships must come out towards the viewer, and florals and scenics must be designed to go up and down. This is limiting. These elongated dimensions call for a good deal of foreshortening. Only figures are somewhat suited to tall cards, which leads us back to studio cards. Most studio cartoons are flat, two-dimensional figures that, along with gag lines, are easy to read in these otherwise unusual proportions. For a comparison, see Figure 10-8.

Chapter Six

Finishing and Folding

Figure 6-1 This multi-fold Japanese screen by Ogata Korin (1658–1716) has been beautifully redesigned as a card. Courtesy of H. George Caspari, Inc. and the Freer Gallery of Art, Smithsonian Institution, Washington, D.C.

FINISHING

Finishing is the term used commonly to describe many of the processes involved in card production. The majority of these procedures are really supplementary activities meant to enhance a card's value, rather than actually finish a card. The primary processes include die cutting, embossing, leaf, bake, and laminating. Each finishing process adds additional expenses to a company's budget, so all such activities are carefully considered. Normally, the less expensive cards receive the least attention.

Some forms of finishing actually do protect the finished design. *Laminating* and *varnishing* are two of these. *Glue tipping*, where exposed parts of a multifolded card are glued together, is another example. Die-cut cards are especially prone to rack damage, and glueing together the weakest areas can give needed protection.

Different finishing activities are often combined on more expensively-priced cards, anniversary designs being one example. Silver and gold leaf (or bake) are frequently found on such cards. Longer anniversaries call for more value. Nearly all twenty-five-year anniversary cards incorporate more than just silver leaf applications. They will likely receive embossing, insert pages, and an inside spot design as well.

As mentioned, less expensively-priced cards normally receive fewer applications, but there is one common exception to this. Cards that sell exceptionally well when first released are often released again the following year or in subsequent years. There are different terms for this; one is *rehashing*. Figure 6-2 shows a *proof* (an

Figure 6-2
This quick sketch by Ron Lister was done with ink and dyes and has sold better than any other design by the author. It was reissued several years in a row. Used by permission of Norcross-Rust Craft Divisions of Windsor Communications Group, Inc.

uncorrected color sample) of what has probably been my most successful card to date. This design was done with liquid dyes and ink. It took no more than two hours to paint and yet has been rehashed at least three times since it was first issued. Because the publisher only had to pay for the artwork and color separation once, they were able to put a little money into it upon reissue. Each time this card was rehashed, it was given a slightly new format along with a new paper stock. Gold leaf or embossing are often added to rehashed designs; however, this particular card did not seem to need either.

Another reason for adding finishes to rehashed cards is to disguise them. Buyers will recognize cards that are reissued, and sales may drop off. As a result, I have in my samples box a number of the same designs with various borders and applications. They also range in size, format, and paper stock. Because all paper stocks accept ink in different ways, it is interesting to see just how different the same design can appear on various papers.

Die Cutting

All cards must be shaped either externally or internally by die cutting. This can mean cutting the stock perimeter in a regular 90° angle or cutting it in almost any irregular shape desired. The interior of a card can be cut and shaped using the same methods. There are two basic procedures used in die cutting. When cutting the outside edges of a card, or shaping an envelope, a *hollow die* is used. Hollow dies are similar to a cookie cutter. The process involves pressing the die through large stacks of paper at a time.

A *steel-rule die cut* involves bending a strip of steel to a desired shape and jigsawing it into a block of plywood, with the cutting edge projecting one-quarter inch above the wood. The die is then locked into the platen of a die-cutting press, and the paper stock is cut as it is fed through the press. Die cutting can be done on a platen press or a flat-bed cylinder press (see Chapter Thirteen).

Cutting and shaping the outside edge of a card in an irregular fashion is common. Normally, the die edge follows the outer perimeter of a design that has been especially planned to include an irregular shape. Figure 6-3 is a good

Figure 6-3
A strong but simple die cut can greatly
enhance a card. Copyright 1980 by
American Greetings Corp.,
75C 609-57E

example of a die-cut card. This juvenile card has been carefully planned to include a simple die-cut edge along two of its sides. The addition of the heart allows the cut to continue across the top of the card and at the same time creates ample room for the caption. This card's die cut has been well-designed. The outer shape is interesting, achieving the primary purpose of the process. However, the cut edges have been kept simple. Deep-set or fancy cuts can render a card helpless against outside damages.

Note: Outer-edge die cuts of this type are indicated for review by placing a cut mat over the actual design that simulates what the card will look like after it has been cut and shaped. The card itself is painted to usual (full) dimensions. This allows the publisher the option of not using the die cut in the future.

Embossing

Embossing is one of the more expensive processes. It produces a design with an actual relief (raised) surface. The old method of using two dies has been largely eliminated. Today, embossing is achieved by pressing the paper stock between a brass female die and a male counter or bed, both of which are mounted in register, with a printed image, onto a press. The male counter is an impression made from the female die and is the only raised area on the bed of the press. This insures that only the desired areas of the design will be embossed when the paper is stamped between the die and the bed.

Embossing on a blank paper surface is termed *blind embossing*. This creates a beautiful low relief effect free from any actual drawing or painting.

Leaf Stamps

Adding leaf—gold, silver, or bronze—is one more way of giving extra value to a design. Like embossing, the cost depends on how much of an area gets the application. A 3″ × 5″ leaf area is considerably less expensive than a 4″ × 5″ area. For this reason, an art director or line planner may indicate to the artist precisely how much leaf can be used in a specific design. Sometimes, this includes only enough space for the caption to be done in leaf. In Figure 6-4, however, leaf has been planned as a major portion of the design.

Leaf stamping is a letterpress process which directly involves embossing. The stamp is etched out of brass and is hand-finished. It is then mounted on a *ribbon*, which is a sheet of gold or whatever color foil has been chosen. Besides gold, silver, and bronze, there are a variety of colored foils available. The ribbon is then applied under heat and pressure in an embossing process. Again, only one die is used, and the stock is fed between it and a flat bed or counter.

Thermography (Colored Bakes)

Gold, silver, or any basic color of ink can be added to a design by *thermography*, which simply means "applied under heat." If a company desires a colored bake in the design, they will specify which color to the artist. The artist indicates bake by doing a simulation on prepared acetate with the chosen color of ink. A reproduction artist will later translate that acetate drawing (which is usually linear) into black and white for the printer.

In the actual process, the ink spreads out and dries on top of the paper stock. This gives the card a raised, letterpress effect.

Note: Because bakes are literally melted onto a card's surface, they tend to flatten or spread out, making it difficult to achieve very fine lines and details. Figure 6-5 displays a design before and after bake was added. This card used brown bake which I simulated for review by using brown paint on acetate. The paint was slightly diluted and applied to a Hunt's artist pen nib.

Figure 6-4
Seasons Greetings. The central design and caption have both been printed in gold leaf, which makes a strong impression. Courtesy of Sidney J. Burgoyne & Sons, Inc., Philadelphia, PA.

Figure 6-5
By Ron Lister. The photo on the right shows an uncorrected proof. the finished card on the left is the same design with a linear *bake* added. Used by permission of Norcross-Rust Craft Divisions of Windsor Communications Group, Inc.

Flocking

Flocking is not as common as it was only a few years ago, but it can still be found on cards, silk-screened shirts, and wallpapers. In this process, very small pieces of fiber are forced into the ink while it is still wet. The end of the fiber embeds in the ink and, when dry, gives the treated image an unusual texture and surface.

Laminating and Varnishing

Laminating refers to the bonding or attaching of two or more materials together. It is used in many forms of graphic art. In cards, a clear plastic is applied as a protective coating. The plastic overlay gives the design a glossy sheen and is a nice finishing touch.

Varnishing places a coating on the surface that will resist heat, water, or other elements which could damage the paper. Varnish can be placed on the stock using a press if the entire surface is to be coated.

FOLDING

The way a card is folded has a direct bearing on the design of the card. It also gives, or takes away, some of its basic strength. The latter is an important consideration in all paper products, from cards to package and carton design. A product that gets damaged on the racks will not sell.

Besides card strength, folds help to enhance appearance. The variety of folds is quite large, ranging from simple single folds to multi-folded pop-up designs.

Note: Nearly all paper products are folded by first *scoring* the paper stock. Scoring leaves a crease in the paper that insures an accurate fold. Cards are scored with a round-edged die called a *scoring rule*, which creases but never cuts into the paper's surface. When scoring your own cards, be sure to use a blunt edge, never a sharp one, and fold against the score to get an embossed (raised) edge.

Single and French Folds

The vast majority of cards are either single- or double-folded. Double folds are termed *French folds* and are often identified on spec sheets by the marking *F.F.* Single folds are marked *S.F.*

Current trends are toward simple designs, and single folds are as popular now as ever before. But while they are the least expensive to produce, they are also the least protected from rack damage. Because of this, single-folded cards are generally printed on heavier, stronger pa-

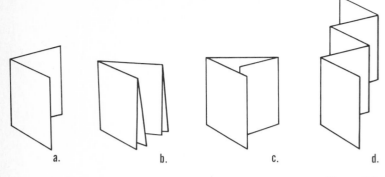

pers called *cover stocks*. They are often laminated or plastic-coated for extra protection as well.

French folds are still the most popular choice for larger, more expensive, and more elaborate designs. Softer, more delicate papers can be used, which directly enhances market value. There is no rule that prohibits larger cards from being single-folded. It simply is not as common.

Note: All cards are folded with approximately $1/16''$ less area on the back cover to insure proper folding. If this is not done, any error in folding will show up visibly along the open side of the front. Painting a bleed along the folded and cutting or open sides of a card accomplishes the same type of protection.

Short Folds

A *short fold* is a slight variation to either a single- or double-folded card. The cover's opening edge is cut short by $1/4''$, letting the inside page show through. Often the inside edge, which is the right-hand side, is treated with a band of gold or silver leaf. When the card is in a folded position, the leaf border will appear to be applied to the cover.

Cards can be short-folded in a variety of ways. Sometimes, the cover design is die cut to show more of the same design from the inside page. This cut can be straight or irregular depending on the look intended.

Note: Short folds are seldom cut less than $1/4''$. Anything narrower would show up if the card were not perfectly folded.

Short Fold Variations

Instead of a card actually being short-folded to reveal a leaf or color border inside, it can be simulated by placing a leaf border directly on the cover and not short-cutting the paper.

Another, perhaps more common, type of short fold is a different die cut termed a *deckle edge*. This process gives the card's cut edge (along the right side) a torn, rippled appearance. This can be simulated for review by tearing or roughly cutting the appropriate edge of the mat which covers the design.

Z Folds

Z folds are divided into three successively smaller sections: cover, middle, and back page. A Z-folded card (see Figure 6-7) with a $4^{8}/_{16}''$ cover width would have a middle page of $4^{7}/_{16}''$ and a back page of $4^{6}/_{16}''$. Again, this is done for protection against any flaws in the folding. In Figure 6-7, the scene is carried on through the inner sections, with each page being nearly a self-contained cover. Note also that each page allows ample caption room.

From a designer's standpoint, the cover must include enough of the composition to interest the viewer. The cover layout should lead the eye casually towards the inside pages but should still stand out as the most important segment. Be sure not to chop off too much of the subject at the first fold. If a tree lines the right-hand area, allow most of it to show on the front. Never place that tree on the middle page, leaving only a branch or two hanging out onto the cover.

Note: Any bake, leaf, or embossing that appears on the cover of a Z-folded card must stop sufficiently short of the folding edge, where it would crack or peel. Normally, cost prohibits continuing such applications on the inside divisions anyway.

U, Gate, and Accordian Folds

A *U fold* is a three-sectioned card that opens outward instead of sideways, and one side at a time.

A *gate fold* is a split U fold. The card opens in the middle, or off-center, instead of one whole side at a time.

An *accordian fold* is a Z-folded type card with more than three sections, normally four or five. See Figure 6-1.

Glue-Tipped Cards

Glue-tipped refers to the process of glueing together two or more sections of a card. It is often done to give French-folded die cuts added pro-

Figure 6-7
A Christmas Z fold painted on a gesso-coated illustration board, by Ron Lister. Used by permission of Norcross-Rust Craft Divisions of Windsor Communications Group, Inc.

Figure 6-8
St. Basil's by Ted Naos. This beautiful card is basically a U fold, but the intricate die cutting adds a new dimension to the way the card folds together. Copyright by and courtesy of the artist.

Figure 6-9
Poppy by Ron Lister. This is a rather large inside spot.
Normally, inside designs appear on the left hand side
of the fold.

tection. Without glueing, the individual papers might peel apart from one another. Inserts are glue-tipped as well, generally to the inside of the cover.

More Advanced Folds

There are numerous other folds: *hinged folds*, which open from the top of the card; *moving wheels*; and a wide variety of ingenious *pop-up* designs. Such folds rely on specific design plans provided by the card publisher.

INSIDE DESIGNS AND INSERTS

In past years, the majority of cards had some type of inside art, either a small vignette of the cover subject, termed an *inside spot* (see Figure 6-9), or a decorative border on an *insert*. An insert is basically a card within a card, a single- or French-folded paper containing a verse with an inside spot or border. Inserts are generally made 1/4″ smaller than the cover dimensions.

Single-folded cards do not, as a rule, carry inside art because it would require printing on both sides of the card. If such art does appear inside a single-fold design, it is usually a line drawing done in one color and *screened down* to a soft vignette.

CONCLUSIONS

Today, the expense of producing even basic card formats is quite high. Rising overhead in all areas of production and marketing have sharply affected the card field. Only special cards and promotional designs receive anywhere near the special attention cards as a whole once got. Still, an endless variety of forms does exist if we look at the entire market—although not in the large numbers of past years.

In the end, it is money that dictates to a company what special finishes a design will get, and it is the company's responsibility to give their artists any special instructions needed to carry out those plans.

Chapter Seven

Styles and Techniques

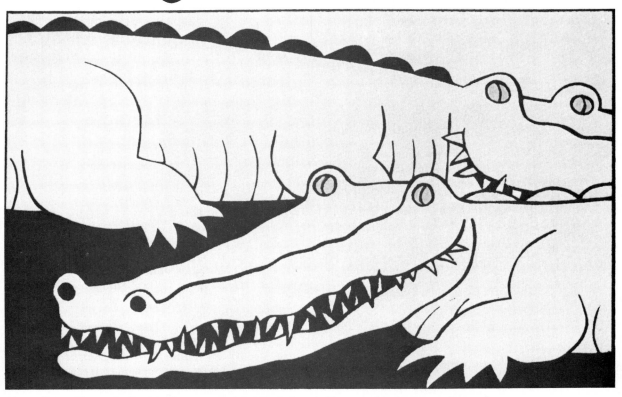

Figure 7-1 *Alligators* by Patricia Overmoyer. A boldly designed silkscreen that does not rely on color. Copyright by and courtesy of the Patsy Co.

DEVELOPING A STYLE

Nearly all artists try to develop a personal style, an individual approach that will bring recognition of special skills and talents. In the greeting card industry, this is not an easy task. Besides the many artists competing for the same markets, companies are competing as well. They too are trying to develop or maintain their own style or look, and they rely on their artists to conform to the company plan. Even the large publishers have a tight overview of their entire line of prod-

ucts. They like to assign specific designs to certain designers to insure the card lines do not overlap or deviate too far from the norm. This makes good business sense, but what is good for the company may not be good for the artist. Personal ambitions often conflict.

In the conventional card field, the choices are limited. We can develop our own style and try to find a publisher who likes it, or we can alter our personal style to fit in with a particular company's look. This situation would be discouraging if it were not for the many companies in need of artwork. Beyond this, if our artistic aims still do not fit in anywhere, we can always start our own company. It would not be the first time that was done.

On the positive side, there are card publishers that openly encourage personal expression, companies that buy cards exhibiting a wide range of styles and techniques. Renaissance on the East Coast, Recycled Paper Products in the Midwest, and Paper Moon Graphics on the West Coast are but a few of these. Each has a policy of looking at a variety of personal expressions. Perhaps the best example of this is the story of Recycled Papers in Chicago and Sandra Boynton.

─────────────────────────────────

Profile:
Recycled Papers and Sandra Boynton

This profile is unique in two ways. It not only chronicles the story of the most successful card company in recent history, but also the most successful individual as well. Recycled Paper Products (R.P.P.) dates back only to 1971, and Sandra Boynton's association with

Figure 7-3
Don't let the turkeys get you down by Sandra Boynton. Cup design courtesy of Recycled Paper Products, Inc.

the company began some five years later, yet the figures are staggering. R.P.P. grossed $600,000 in sales in 1974. By 1980, with Boynton's input, that figure rose to $25 million, or approximately 150 million cards and assorted products (R.P.P. also makes wrapping paper, T-shirts, calendars, buttons, and coffee mugs). (See Figure 7-3.) They are also beginning to produce stuffed animals based on Boynton characters.

Recycled Paper Products was cofounded by Michael L. Keiser and Philip Friedman. Today, as vice presidents (the company has no president), they are directly responsible for the great success of their company. Keiser believes that Recycled Paper Products may already be the third largest seller of card products in the United States, although he adds that such status is still "hard to verify." The people at R.P.P. are proud of their current position. Being third, even a distant third, in so short a time in such a large industry is quite an accomplishment.

In talking about the top three or four manufacturers, it should be pointed out that Recycled Paper Products is fundamentally different from Hallmark and American Greetings. R.P.P. represents the advance of the smaller companies into the larger card market. Not really trendy in concept, R.P.P. cards are still considerably less conservative than the cards of most large companies. Now that Recycled Paper Products is established, will things change? "No," says Keiser, "we are just as risk oriented, if not more so. We are always looking for new ideas, new artists."

Since 1980, Recycled Paper Products has continued its phenomenal growth. Good production standards and marketing account for much of their success, but in this case, there is also Sandra Boynton (see

Figure 7-2
Wishing you all the charm of the season by Sandra Boynton. Courtesy of Recycled Paper Products, Inc.

Figures 8-6 and 9-10). It is hard to believe that Boynton cards and products actually account for one-third of Recycled Paper Product's total sales. In hindsight, it is easy to recognize Boynton's immense talent and obvious market value, but when she was just starting out in the mid-1970s, she had to prove herself just like any newcomer. Boynton insists she could not have made it without Recycled Paper Products, claiming she was not particularly interested in the business end of the product. She knew, as do most of us, that it is very difficult to run a successful business and art studio simultaneously. The point is that success at this level is seldom the product of just one person's efforts, even if that one person is Sandra Boynton.

After graduating from Yale in 1974, Boynton began to make gift cards, having 60,000 cards printed by her uncle. She hand-painted each one, and did all the packaging and distribution by herself. Later, she was introduced to Recycled Paper Products, and the story becomes almost a fairy tale of good fortune, but not without some initial difficulties. Boynton negotiated with Recycled Paper Products for a full year to achieve a substantial royalty clause in her contract. Eventually, the partnership was sealed and has been going strong ever since. In 1980 alone, Boynton sold 55 million cards through Recycled Paper Products. Her best designs sell as many as 50,000 per month, and there is no end in sight. Her future plans are to design as many as 500 cards a year for R.P.P.

With such a partnership, who knows how far Recycled Paper Products and Sandra Boynton can go?

TECHNIQUES AND STYLES

In developing an individual style, we often favor certain forms, subjects, and techniques. Frequently, a specific technique is responsible for a distinctive style, but not always. The styles of Matisse and Gaugin, who were excellent designers, are easily recognizable whether we are looking at a print, a drawing, or an oil painting. We can see in each work that part of the design which tells us "This is the way Gaugin saw" or "This is the way Matisse felt." This is an important aspect to consider when trying to develop a personal style. Different subjects may be best depicted with different techniques and materials, but remember that technique is only a part of style.

Note: Technique and style are both rather general terms which overlap considerably. Today, there is no one style or trend that must be adhered to. However, the last few years have seen a shift towards flat, graphic designing (see Chapter One).

For the sake of clarity, I have categorized all current styles into three broad classifications: *graphic*, *semi-graphic*, and *painterly*. Within these categories, I have outlined some of the most common techniques and media used.

Flat-Graphic Techniques

The term *graphic* implies a visual surface which appears to be flat or two-dimensional. Graphic techniques were not generally popular in Western art until the mid-nineteenth century when Japanese woodblock prints began to appear in numbers (see Figure 5-7). In cards, graphic designing has just recently reached a new popularity. There are numerous techniques and media used to attain a flat surface. Any medium, for

Figure 7-4
This strong graphic design by Jean V. O'Brien makes excellent use of two dimensional space. Reprinted with the permission of Gibson Greeting Cards, Inc., with all rights reserved.

GO PLACIDLY AMID THE NOISE AND THE HASTE, AND REMEMBER WHAT PEACE THERE MAY BE IN SILENCE

instance, that can achieve flat, even tones and minimal brush strokes is suited to graphic styles. Figure 1-7 shows a Hallmark floral where the wild flowers stand out from the dark background areas not because of any three-dimensional illusions, but through conventional graphic techniques. In this case, the different forms are separated by color, value contrasts, and, most importantly, *outlining*. It is the outline of each rose leaf and stem that helps to denote the forms and to give detail. Notice, too, in most graphic-oriented cards, negative areas take on greater importance to the overall design.

The majority of graphic techniques are achieved with designers' gouache. Water-colors and liquid dyes can be used as well, but because of their transparent nature, they tend to be less suited for producing even, flat tones. Cameras

and laser scanners, which do most of today's color separations, are able to pick out even the smallest flaws or inconsistencies in color, just the type of inconsistencies common to the more transparent media.

Besides designers' colors, there are several other media well suited to graphic designing. Woodcuts, linocuts, and silkscreens are among the best. These three media are also favorite choices for artists who are producing their own cards. Silkscreening is particularly good for achieving heavy, opaque colors which can be reproduced on a variety of surfaces from cards to T-shirts. (For more on these printing methods, see Chapter Fourteen.)

Because most graphic styles involve the use of outlines, renderings are normally somewhat tight or controlled. One general exception is stu-

Figure 7-5
You're Irresistible by Maryann Cocca. Courtesy of Marcel and Company, Everett, MA. Copyright 1982 by Maryann Cocca.

dio cards. In cartooning, hard outlines are common, but the drawings must be loose. Cartoon lines have to be carefully controlled but must still retain a feeling of movement and energy. I suspect most people who have not tried cartooning do not fully understand the difficulty of doing this.

Outside of cartooning, loose, graphic styles can still be found. They are just not as common. The bird of peace, shown in Figure 7-6, has been beautifully sketched. It is a loose gesture drawing that simply and quickly conveys movement and energy in a refreshing way.

Semi-Flat Techniques

Semi-flat technique refers to any design with a limited modulation of color and value contrasts, a card that appears to be neither flat nor fully three-dimensional. Such designs can be tightly drawn or loosely sketched. My Thanksgiving card, Figure 7-7, displays a loosely-drawn subject I would term *semi-graphic*. The technique involves

Figure 7-6
Bird of Peace. This nice *gesture* drawing was one of the first cards ever published by Recycled Paper Products. Courtesy of Recycled Paper Products, Inc.

Figure 7-7
By Ron Lister. Although the colors in this design do modulate to some extent, they were not used to create a three dimensional effect. The space remains semiflat. Used by permission of Norcross-Rust Craft Divisions of Windsor Communications Group, Inc.

two media: ink and liquid dyes. First, the dyes are laid down on a slightly wetted board surface. The colors (reds, yellows, and greens) are allowed to bleed or run. This creates variety in both color concentration and general value contrasts. Next, a sepia ink drawing is superimposed directly over the color work. When the ink is dry, a few chosen areas are wetted for a second time, again allowing a controlled amount of color to bleed. The partially washed-out sketch and bleeded colors both give this card its loose appearance.

Another example of a semi-flat technique is shown in Figure 5-3. Here, the rendering is much tighter than my Thanksgiving number, but the style is still semi-graphic. The two cars and enlarged hood ornament have been carefully drawn.

Each object has been outlined, but within those outlines, the colors and values modulate to some extent. This modulation gives the design a partially three-dimensional look. However, the outlining and clear definition of each object do not add to, but rather detract from, any three-dimensional illusion. As objects go back in space, they lose definition. This is called *aerial perspective*. Yet in this design, only the slightest trace of aerial perspective can be found, in the drawing of tires.

Semi-graphic styles can be achieved with a variety of media. Gouache, watercolors, dyes, markers, practically all color media, can be adapted. Transparent watercolors and dyes are, however, most frequently used.

THE PAINTERLY APPROACH

Painterly is almost a self-explanatory term. In cards, it pertains to designs which make visible use of the painter's craft. This includes visible brush strokes and textures. Painterly styles are generally associated with the traditional mode of showing three-dimensional illusion. I am referring here to conventional or representational

types of cards, where scenes, still life objects, and figures are all depicted in the older, traditional way.

Painterly styles do not have to be representational. They can just as well be semi- or totally abstract (see Figure 7-8). It all depends on the approach and the purpose at hand. I used to design many cards for the European and Australian markets and was always aware of the different attitudes of their art directors and line planners towards designing. Both the English and the Australians appreciate the more conservative, representational types of designs, which are often more painterly as well. Of course, there are exceptions to this, but in general, trends in the United States fluctuate more than their counterparts in Europe and elsewhere. The past decades have seen numerous styles come and go. Competition and the America love of novelty have created a large turnover.

Basic Painterly Techniques

When we think of painting, we most often think of oil painting. Since the days of Jan Van Eyck, oils have been cherished for their wonderful range

Figure 7-8
By Shu Dick Ju. This *painterly* design is actually a fine arts watercolor scaled down to a calendar format. Used by permission of Norcross-Rust Craft Divisions of Windsor Communications Group, Inc.

Figure 7-9

Ducks at a Pond by Ron Lister. Oil painting is seldom used in commercial paper products, though this one was reproduced as a calendar page. Used by permission of Norcross-Rust Craft Divisions of Windsor Communications Group, Inc.

of effects. The Impressionist painters Monet, Pissarro, and Renoir made great use of strokes and textures to create their atmospheric pictures. Their aims may have been scientific, but it is their vivid colors and visible brush strokes that please us today. My own painting "Ducks at a Pond," Figure 7-9, was done in oils with an Impressionist technique. In this painting, I tried to make good use of my brush strokes; the paint was laid on quickly and heavily.

Oils are great fun and are well-suited for accomplishing a wide range of effects; unfortunately, they are hard to reproduce in printing. The unevenness of the pigment, the semi-reflective paint surface, and the various degrees of opacity are qualities the separation camera has trouble with. So, in cards we are more often asked to simulate oil techniques than to actually paint them. My oil painting of the ducks was used in a fine arts calendar. However, I have had relatively few oils printed as cards or calendars. Instead, I have simulated oils on quite

a few occasions. One technique for doing this is shown in Figure 6-7. I first primed a sheet of illustration board with gesso. (Gesso is the primer or undercoat used to cover untreated canvas for oil painting. It hardens, leaving visible brush strokes in the surface.) In this Z-fold landscape, gouache colors are used over the gesso. The gouache sinks into the primer, but the brush strokes remain visible. The effect is similar to oil painting.

Note: This technique also has the advantage of having a good reworking surface. The gesso, with gouache or without, can be easily erased or sanded down to remove any undesired areas or details.

There are many other techniques which involve watercolors and gouache in a painterly fashion. Watercolors on watercolor papers achieve some handsome painterly qualities (see Figure 7-9). Transparent watercolors are absorbed quickly and unevenly into a watercolor paper surface, and this leaves visible drying marks. Re-

75

Figure 7-10
Golden Retrievers by Anatoly Dverin. Both a loose wash and dry brush strokes were first put down. Individual strokes were then added to complete the "indication" of hair. Used by permission of Norcross-Rust Craft Divisions of Windsor Communications Group, Inc.

member, too, when gouache is thinned out, it acts very much the same as transparent watercolor. It is a matter of intent on the part of the artist.

DRAWING STYLES

The brush is a very versatile instrument. With a fine point, it can be used to draw as a pencil might. Figure 7-10 shows such a technique. A fine brush tip was employed to create a tight, controlled still life, with the brush acting as a drawing instrument. The brush was also used to simulate the hair of the golden retrievers. Individual fine-line strokes and wider, dry brush strokes were both used to accomplish this effect.

Drawing styles are as numerous as subjects. Some subjects need tight rendering, while others might require a loose, free hand. As a general rule, it is best to be able to handle a brush and pen in all these various ways. Practice drawing on acetate as well. The smooth plastic surface is great for drawing on with both pen or brush. Some graphic styles use acetate, while nearly all cartoon styles require it.

Cartoon Styles

Cartooning relies perhaps more on good drawing technique than any other card form. Colors are normally bright and intense. Semi-transparent watercolors and dyes are employed to paint in the forms of the design, but, unlike conventional cards, studio cartooning relies mostly on the linear drawing which is placed on the top of the wash tones. Usually, this drawing is done on a separate acetate overlay.

The art of caricature can be seen in conventional cards as well. Figure 7-11 is a card from a series of designs by Tom Cante. Here dyes were used on illustration board with a pencil line added directly over the color work.

Humorous and juvenile cards also involve cartooning, though in a more conventionally cute fashion than studio cards (see Figures 6-3 and 7-2). Humorous and juvenile cards both use common card formats, whereas studio cards are long and narrow by comparison. (For more on cute designs, see Chapter Eight.)

Studio Cards

In cards, the purest forms of cartooning are the *studio* lines. These are the most illustrative in approach and rely heavily on the verse or *gag line* to complete the picture. In most card lines drawing and colors are normally integrated on the board. In studio cards, the color work is usually separated. The line work is done with black ink on an acetate overlay. Figure 3-7 is a page taken from a friendship gift book on things to do while you are in the hospital. While the format is not the typical tall dimension of most studio cards, the technique is. Basic blues, reds, and yellows were painted first, and the line work was done on acetate. (Also see Figure 10-8.)

Figure 7-11
Unlike studio cards, both the colored dyes and the pencil lines in this Tom Cante design were applied directly on the illustration board. Used by permission of Norcross-Rust Craft Divisions of Windsor Communications Group, Inc.

Profile:
Ray Medici, Studio Cartoonist

Ray Medici is an established studio-card designer. He studied advertising design and illustration at the New England School of Art during the 1960s and is currently freelancing full-time for Gibson Cards.

Ron: Did you learn cartooning from anyone in particular?

Ray: No, primarily from my favorite cartoonists in the comic strips. As a kid, I loved Al Capp. I think Mort Drucker is very good. He's in *Mad* magazine. I like Gahan Wilson and Lou Marak. He's a Hallmark studio artist. Paul Coker, Jr., is a Hallmark studio artist, too.

Ron: What gave you the idea to do studio cards instead of other forms of cartooning?

Ray: I think the idea of a steady job helped. If you're a cartoonist, a lot of times it's on a freelance basis and it's not steady money. Also, the greeting card format was nice. It was like telling a little story.

Ron: Have you ever done any gag writing?

Ray: No.

IN THE HOSPITAL...
When germs come to VISIT,
your DOCTOR knows BEST
so take all of your PILLS
and get plenty
of REST.

And you'll SOON be RID of
that UNWELCOME GUEST.

GET WELL SOON

Figure 7-12

This studio Z fold by Ray Medici shows the close relationship between verse and design found in most studio cards. Used by permission of Norcross-Rust Craft Divisions of Windsor Communications Group, Inc.

Ron: How does color in studio cards compare with color in conventional cards?

Ray: It's looser. It's a wash type of approach as opposed to a gouache or opaque approach. Right now, I use primarily dyes, some watercolors, too.

Ron: Are studio cards ever done with P.M.S. colors?

Ray: Only the backgrounds are dropped in with P.M.S. colors. In the old days, when Paul Coker—by the way, Paul Coker, Jr., was the first artist to come up with the neuter character. He was the first to come up with the wacky studio approach. Before Coker, it was more of a cute-type of approach on studio cards.

Ron: You separate your color work, right?

Ray: Yes, I do most of my line work on an acetate overlay. Recent trends, though, are to use colored pencils in kind of a sketchy type of outline, and that's done directly on the artwork.

Sandra Boynton is very important in the new styles. She broke the ground. Today, the trend is toward small, witty-type drawings, not drawings that fill up the whole card. They're using vat-dyed papers (muted, colored papers) more often these days for that Boynton-style background. All you do is pick out a color and do your line work on an overlay and put your watercolors right on the paper. It's very absorbent, so that saves you the trouble of dropping in backgrounds.

Ron: Have you ever done your own color separation?

Ray: Yes, I've done that, but no more these days, thank God.

Ron: What special training can an outsider get for studio cards?

Ray: A good cartoon course, especially one showing a variety of cartoon styles. Drawing courses, too; that's still very important. I think nowadays the drawing aspect is kind of glossed over by a lot of the young kids at school. They don't take the time for the drawing.

Ron: Do you have any tips for those starting out?

Ray: I'd say look at the trends. Look at what's out there right now before you try anything. The humorous and studio departments are changing their look almost every two or three years. Keep up with the trends and send out a lot of work to a lot of places. You have to be up to the minute with your look, your style.

P.M.S. COLORS

Numerous ink manufacturers put out sample books showing the colors they offer. This allows artists and art directors the opportunity to visualize a finished product before it is printed and to separate colors by eye.

For a card designer, the most familiar color book is the P.M.S. sample book published by Pantone, Inc. (55 Knickerbocker Road, Moonachie, New Jersey 07074). The P.M.S. refers to Pantone Matching Systems. The book displays nearly 900 individual ink colors and is made up of long, loose-leafed cards. Each one displays seven 2″ x ³/₄″ color swatches. Each card also fans out to show as many colors as desired. All the colors are shown twice, on both coated and uncoated paper stock. This system of using predetermined colors is called *precepted art*.

Precepted Art

In precepted art, the artist is directed to use certain colors from the P.M.S. sample book. It is the line planner (see Chapter Eleven) or the art director who normally decides which colors and how many are to be used. Once this is done, the artist designs the card by simulating the chosen colors with designers' colors. The colors can be screened down (softened by percentages, that is, 90%, 80%, and so on) but never mixed to create new colors. Figure 9-5 shows a poppy design gift wrap, which uses three precepted colors (orange, blue and green). The wrap is designed by matching the colors specifically for the review board. Once it is accepted, a working mechanical is made in black and white for the printer. The printer then refers to the P.M.S. color chosen in the beginning.

In cards, wallpapers, and gift wraps, several P.M.S. colors are normally used at one time. In such cases, a separate black and white mechanical is produced to show the placement of each color. Later on, the company can change any or all of the colors in the design by simply choosing new ones from the sample book.

Note: P.M.S. colors are utilized most often in special situations. They are frequently used for dropping in backgrounds on humorous and studio cards as discussed. Also, P.M.S. colors are used almost exclusively in designing party goods, that is, napkins, paper cups, placemats, table cloths, and so on.

PHOTOGRAPHY

Photography as Technique

Of all the various techniques associated with cards and paper products, photography holds a special place. There seem to be few artists who are not fond of cameras. Shooting film is great fun, and we like to think our photographs have a certain quality and interest that reaches beyond mere personal enjoyment. For years, I have taken reference pictures throughout the parks and floral shops in my area (see Figure 4-2). I believe my photography and developing methods have reached a fairly professional level. I did manage to shoot and enlarge all of the photographs in this book, yet I realize my limitations. There can be a great deal of difference between an artistic photograph and an artistic photograph which is also saleable. Beyond that, photography requires a full-time effort. The market is very popular, and the competition is amazingly tough. Many who have an artistic eye with the camera simply lack the high degree of technical expertise and knowledge needed to be successful commercially. If this sounds like a warning, it should. I strongly suggest doing some research before jumping into this field. The following pages should help to provide some of the necessary groundwork for making any decisions about a career in photography.

Photographic Subjects

When considering subject matter, two things should come to mind. The first concerns the decision of what to photograph, and the second, the creative choices that evolve after a subject has been chosen. Most of us have a basic idea of which subjects are commercially viable: landscapes and scenics, wildlife and domestic animals, florals and still lifes, and so on. Photographing people is more complex. There is a constant market for quality shots of celebrities, living or dead. Pictures of Marilyn Monroe are selling as well today as they did back in the 1960s. Sports figures and sports situations are another fairly consistent market, but beyond that,

Figure 7-13
Photography in cards is intensely competitive. Good shots are not usually enough. Only great ones generally make it.
Courtesy of Hallmark Cards, Inc.

things become uncertain. The demand for clothed figures, nudes, and portraits is very limited.

In cards, loving couples and solitary figures on the beach or campus are used for special occasions. These figures are normally shot with filters to create a hazy, soft, and slightly out-of-focus effect. This is done for two reasons. One is to give the situation atmosphere, and the other is to allow the viewer to fill in the faces and ages of those in the photograph. Such techniques give the card a wider consumer base.

Of the other subjects mentioned, landscapes, scenics, and animals are always in demand, but nearly everyone loves to take these types of pictures, which makes for a very tight market. This is especially true where cute animal photographs are concerned. The market is so flooded that an artist who wishes to contribute must stay right on top of current demands. One month, there may be a demand for puppies, and the next month, they may be looking only for bear cubs. Anyone interested in this area must be willing to shoot many rolls of film.

My advice in approaching the subject is to be professional from the start. For instance, if you wish to sell landscapes, go out and observe what the best landscapes are and who publishes them. Look at a Sierra Club calendar or card. Notice the clarity, scope, angle of lens, density, and composition of the photos. Try to duplicate those qualities in your own work. When you can objectively say you have captured a number of landscapes with equal clarity and control, *then* approach the art directors with your work. The standards in this industry are often higher than one expects to find.

Having stated several negatives, let us consider why a career in photography might be worth it. First of all, there are many products in need of good photography: cards, postcards, posters, puzzles, games, and wall decors, to mention just a few. Secondly, the professional photographer makes good money doing something which is a lot of fun. Finally, photography is an artistic endeavor that does not require special drawing and painting skills. It is an area where anyone with a good sense of layout and design can learn the necessary technical skills to compete in the field.

Camera Format

Anyone seriously interested in photography must own a good camera and know how to use it in a variety of situations. In the past, large format cameras were the standard. Today, it is merely a luxury to own a $2^1/_4''$ x $2^1/_4''$ Hasselblad, as most companies accept and expect 35 mm. The larger format cameras are still great to use, however, and offer some of the finest-quality work available. A few calendar companies still prefer them, but most companies are now accustomed to seeing the smaller 35 mm format.

Note: Most professionals use Kodachrome film because it takes the sharpest, grain-free 35 mm pictures. Ektachrome may be faster and easier to shoot, but it offers no match in quality.

Color vs. Black and White

Companies prefer to look at and buy color. On the racks, color always outsells black and white. Besides, color can be converted into black and white should the need arise.

Slides

Some companies will look only at slides. Professionally, slides are called *color transparencies* or *color positives*. In general, 35 mm transparencies are accepted everywhere. Companies do not as a rule like to see a mixture of prints and slides, especially prints of different sizes and dimensions. If they see this, they may assume the photographer is not professional. This is not just an art director's whim. Prints made from negatives usually do lose some color and detail, hence the preference for slides.

Selling Photographs

Photographs are purchased in two basic ways. They can be bought from *stock* or *on assignment*. A few card companies still give assignments to professionals they know will capture the required look and feel. For years, the majority of work was purchased this way. Today, however, more money is spent on stock photographs. With this system, the photographer builds up a stockpile of work on a variety of subjects. When a particular need arises, all photos of the desired subject(s) are submitted on speculation. The agency then can choose from an assortment of treatments and pick one they feel comes closest to their expectations. Art directors prefer to have such options whenever possible.

This system has both advantages and dis-

Figure 7-14
Pelicans by Ron Lister. Subtle colors and a good composition make this photograph potential postcard or greeting card quality. But for every photo that "makes" it, there are scores that do not.

advantages for the artist. The major drawback is that a lot of film must be shot in order to sell a few photos. The principal advantage of this system is that it reduces some of the pressure which often accompanies assigned work.

Portfolios

Photographic portfolios must be kept simple and neat. Like conventional card portfolios, they should only include work that has a chance of actually selling. It is better to send your work in batches (small groups) than to show all your work in one large portfolio. Because slides are normally used, photographic batches are often larger than card batches. Still, I would limit the number to twenty or thirty, if possible. Slides can be sent in plastic loose-leafed folders, which are easily purchased at any photographic supply store.

Finding the Market

The *Photographer's Market* is published annually by Writer's Digest of Cincinnati, Ohio. It is the most comprehensive book of its kind, listing a wide variety of selling markets. The book also includes some solid advice about commercial photography in general.

To locate other sources not listed in the *Photographer's Market*, become accustomed to carrying pen and paper. Look at those publishers that are producing photography that appeals to you. Write down any available addresses and make inquiries. Ask the store manager for help, if needed.

When making inquiries to a company or agency, you may wish to ask if there are any special considerations involved in sending a portfolio.

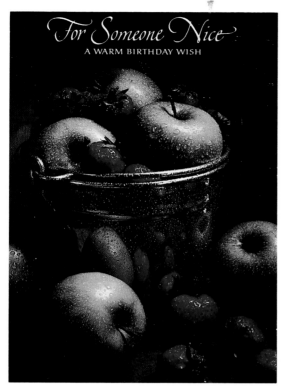

Plate 1
Courtesy of Hallmark Cards Inc.

Plate 2
A Holly Hobbie doll. Copyright 1983
by American Greetings Corp. Designed
by Judy Mitchell for Gorham, licensee. Courtesy of
GORHAM DIVISION OF TEXTRON INC.,
Providence, Rhode Island.

Plate 3
Christmas Bells. Courtesy of Hallmark Cards Inc.

Plate 4
By Ron Lister. The author's first card, painted on a brown paper towel.
Used by permission of Norcross-Rust Craft Divisions of Windsor Communications Group, Inc.

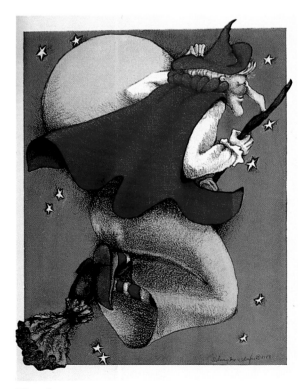

Plate 5
"Witching you a Happy Halloween" (inside caption)
by Sid Stromsdorfer. Copyright by and courtesy of
Renaissance Greeting Cards, Springvale, Maine.

Plate 6
By Nancy Kellerman. Courtesy of Red Farm Studio.

Plate 7
By Anatoly Dverin. Courtesy of
the Paramount Line Inc., Pawtucket, Rhode Island.

Plate 8
"Wishing you all the charm of the season"
(inside caption) by Sandra Boynton. Courtesy of
Recycled Paper Products, Inc., Chicago, Illinois.

Plate 9
By Ron Lister (a detail from a larger design). Courtesy of Red Farm Studio.

Plate 10
By Ron Lister. Courtesy of Red Farm Studio.

Plate 11
By Ron Lister. Used by permission of Norcross-Rust Craft
Divisions of Windsor Communications Group, Inc.

Plate 12
By Ron Lister. Courtesy of Red Farm Studio.

Chapter Eight

Occasions, Holidays, and Subjects

Figure 8-1 By Ron Lister. Used by permission of Norcross-Rust Craft Divisions of Windsor Communications Group, Inc.

OCCASIONS

Greeting cards have always been associated with special events, and though recently we have witnessed a surge in cards without captions or apparent sentiments, these account for only a small percentage of the overall market.

Card lines can be divided into two broad categories. The first group includes seasonal holidays and religious occasions. The second contains the everyday line: birthdays, weddings, anniversaries, and so on.

The Christmas-New Years line is the largest (and oldest) in the industry. It includes gift wraps, ribbon, bows, note cards, party goods, paper gifts, and, of course, cards. There are quite a few companies that publish only Christmas cards. The oldest of these is Sidney J. Burgoyne and Sons of Philadelphia (see Figure 6-4), founded in 1907; however, after seventy-five years of specializing, they are now beginning to market other card lines.

Almost all paper products manufacturers are involved to some degree with the Christmas market. A conservative estimate is that twenty-five percent of this country's entire annual consumer sales occur between early December and January. The card and paper market also soars at this time, and as the general economy tightens, cards appear to replace gifts. So far, the card industry has been recession-proof. With the amount of Christmas inventory being so high, it is nearly impossible for card and paper designers not to be involved.

Most seasonal cards are painted six to ten months ahead of time. So it is common to find yourself painting Santa Claus and his troops, snowy evergreens, and fireplace settings in the

Figure 8-2
The Madonna of the Eucharist by Sandro Botticelli (1444–1510). Reproductions of this great Renaissance masterpiece are currently being produced as Christmas cards. In the past few years, museums have been contributing in ever increasing numbers to the card market. Courtesy of the Isabella Stewart Gardner Museum, Boston, Mass.

Figure 8-3
By Anatoly Dverin. Christmas has perhaps more direct symbolism than any other card line. Courtesy of the Paramount Line, Inc., Pawtucket, R.I.

middle of a summer heat wave. Christmas, like any religious or political holiday, relies heavily on the use of associated subjects and symbolism. Collecting reference for these events must be accomplished several months before painting the cards. So, planning ahead is vital.

Holiday Symbolism

Each holiday is celebrated usually with both literal and symbolic storytelling. Christmas has perhaps more direct symbolism than any other card line. Besides the associated Christian symbols—the cross, the bird of peace, the Trinity, and so forth—there are countless figurative references that have become associated with Christmas. These include holly, mistletoe, cardinals,

poinsettia, and evergreens. Certain colors have also become associated with the season. What would a Christmas card be without reds and greens?

It is impossible to detail all the myriad forms of religious and seasonal symbolism. The Christian church has literally hundreds of its own. However, I suggest researching the proper symbols for each holiday or occasion. It is helpful to know them regardless of how often you choose to use them. Besides, the use of an improper symbol or reference can be embarrassing and costly.

Along these lines, it is important to know how and where to use your subjects. If you are interested in florals, learn as much as you can about them: when they grow, where they grow, what they symbolize, and so on. By learning this, you will also learn where to use certain flowers and where not to as well.

Everyday Cards

This large grouping encompasses a wide variety of personal sentiments from birthday wishes to sympathy and from weddings to divorces. Whatever the event, no matter how small or personal it is, there is probably a card for it. The backbone of the everyday line is, however, the birthday card. Birthday cards are a big seller, and like most everyday cards, they are sold by the month or season. This is not always apparent, but most publishers are well aware of which months the cards will be out on the market and try to design seasonal elements into the designs.

With the advent of so many small card companies in the past decade, there is quite a diversity of everyday cards and special occasion cards. As mentioned, the smaller card producers have filled in gaps and covered areas where the larger companies will not go. This can be seen especially in cards dealing with certain types of humor. In the 1960s, it was unreasonable to think a line of humorous divorce cards could sell. But during the early 1970s, one of the major publishers tried it. They produced two variations: a serious divorce card and a more humorous one. Apparently, the humorous attempts fell short, while the more serious ones did relatively well—well enough that the following year, I was asked to design an entire divorce *promotion* (a promotion being a group of related cards which are

Figure 8-4
"A Thrilling Birthday." Illustrated by
Maryann Cocca. Courtesy of Marcel
and Company, Everett, Mass. © 1982
by M. Cocca.

designed, promoted, and displayed together as
a unit). The point is the larger companies cannot
afford to market certain limited ideas. It remains
for small card producers and individuals to go
after these smaller markets.

THE NO-OCCASION CARD

In actuality, there are very few cards that serve
no occasion. Nearly all cards contain some type
of sentiment, even if it is not explicit. But while
the vast majority of conventional cards are designed for specific occasions, there has been a
noticeable trend towards a more generalized format. Today, there is a large assortment of in-
dividualized cards, cards which express a simple
sentiment and can be sent on a variety of occasions. I am particularly fond of Wallace Tripps's
cards for Pawprints. Tripps characters, such as

the field mouse in Figure 8-5, express a quiet
sentiment without being trite or contrived. The
only caption appears inside and simply reads
"Chin Up."

Another designer whose cards function for
a variety of occasions is Sandra Boynton. Boynton cards (see Figure 8-6) are whimsical state-
ments, accentuated by clever captions that read
almost as slogans. In Boynton cards, the concepts are so well-thought-out that the artwork
can remain minimal and not lose its effectiveness.

Still, no matter how general the sentiment
may be, it is undeniably one of the key selling
points of any card. I have discussed this issue
with a number of independent card producers,
and the general consensus is that cards with definite captions or specific sentiments outsell those
without. Even those who do not like using captions agreed with this.

SUBJECT MATTER

Greeting Card Reality

In this business, subjects are a world within a world. Greeting card subjects are not really intended to reflect the world, just a small portion of it. To this end, all ideas are adapted or created. The card world seldom, if ever, gets involved in the harsher realities of life, areas where the mass media thrive. Instead, our world is one of sunshine, hope, peace, and humor.

The greatest problem for designers is directly related to the sheer magnitude of the competition. Most artists who are ready to begin a commercial career already have an idea of which subjects and styles they prefer to work with. However, the majority of entrants to the industry are not well-prepared to deal with the high standards they are expected to maintain. It is not nearly as difficult to create one good card as it is to create dozens or hundreds of them on a consistent basis. The card market is a sophis-

ticated one, not only on the inside but on the outside as well. Even the public expects a higher standard.

Most people buying cards have a pretty good idea of what to look for and what to expect. More than ever, they are expecting high quality. With regard to subject, it is best if we assume people *do* know something about what they are buying. For instance, those buying floral art often have a sound, basic knowledge of flowers. They may not buy a card that is incorrectly drawn or appears out of season.

From our perspective, this means we need to be more illustrative than in the past. The industry has matured in the last few decades, and artists who do not realize this and adapt are in for some disappointments.

When I first started out as a floral designer, I learned about my subject from a variety of sources, most of which involved only elementary fieldwork. Some subjects are, however, more specialized than others, including religious and humorous cards.

Figure 8-5
Chin Up by Wallace Tripp. A quiet sentiment. Copyright by Wallace Tripp. Courtesy of Pawprints, Inc., Jaffrey, N.H.

Figure 8-6
Ambition knows no bounds by Sandra Boynton. Courtesy of Recycled Paper Products, Inc.

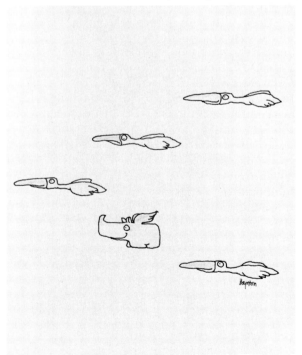

One Solitary Life

Figure 8-7
One Solitary Life by Anatoly Dverin. The traditional story, told here with pastels. Courtesy of the Paramount Line, Inc., Pawtucket, R.I.

Religious Subjects

If there is one category of subject where reference materials abound, it is religious subjects. Both the Christian and Jewish faiths have been well-documented for thousands of years.

It is my experience that religious themes generally call for conventional representation. After all, it has been the story, not the personal expression, that has survived through the ages. As a result, religious products remain somewhat old-fashioned. One area where more contemporary measures can be utilized is symbolism. All religions use symbols to help convey their messages. In fact, symbolism and conventional representation often overlap. Figure 8-8 shows a Jewish design, with a somewhat graphic style. It still relates the necessary message without being too conventionally literal.

Whether using symbolism or conventional representation, all religious products are taken seriously. The histories are rich in the visual arts, making it difficult to interpret the old themes in new ways. Most often, it is a different technique, not an avant-garde style, that helps us the most. In Figure 8-7, by Anatoly Dverin, the traditional story has once again been presented in a conventional fashion. However, this design uses pastel instead of designers colors and is drawn on a dark-brown background instead of a typically light one. This procedure is standard in pastels but not in watercolors. In fact, most watercolor techniques, except for the most opaque, take advantage of the white in the paper. By using pastels, which are best drawn on a neutral tone of paper, Dverin has retold the story in a refreshing way.

It is surprising how few examples can be found in which the story has been visually altered to any great extent. Perhaps the most radical illustrations are those found in the illuminated manuscripts of the British Isles, circa A.D 700. I suggest looking at the Irish "Book of Kells" or the "Lindisfarne Gospel" from Northumberland. Both have appeared in recent publications and can be found in a good art history book. The monks of that period used amazing patience to create their geometric, abstract patterns and designs. The Christian story has seldom been visualized in such a "contemporary" fashion.

Jewish Cards

In discussing Christian designs, I am reminded of a few apparent differences between Christian and Jewish cards. From observation and personal experience, I believe Jewish cards are often less conventional in styling. This has certainly been true of my own involvement. The symbolism and especially the lettering lend themselves to freer interpretations. I have done Jewish cards on rice paper, in markers, and with pastels, and have worked in a variety of techniques and styles.

One more thing should be noted—I always have my symbols and lettering checked for errors.

Figure 8-8
Ron Lister used a stained glass window technique to create a more contemporary effect. This is a card proof. Used by permission of Norcross-Rust Craft Divisions of Windsor Communications Group, Inc.

Juvenile Subjects

Juvenile cards are cute or humorous in concept. The message is very simple, and the artwork is cheerful and lighthearted. The trick to designing juvenile cards lies in the ability to create an imaginary world where chipmunks swing from

Get Well Wishes!

the trees (see Figure 8-9) and furry mice wish us "Happy Birthday" (see Figure 6-3). In these creations, the happiest elements of the real world are transported to the greeting card world. It is a task requiring a keen awareness of children and people, along with the ability to translate those insights into visual terms.

Profile:
Judy Mitchell, Freelance Artist

I first met Judy Mitchell when we were both employed at Rust Craft Publishers. Judy is presently a happy and successful freelance card designer, working from her studio in Natick, Massachusetts. She also does graphic art for the New York Yankees' organization and recently redesigned the Holly Hobbie characters into beautiful dolls for Gorham Textron, Inc., of Providence, Rhode Island (see Figure 9-1).

Judy has always had a flair for cute, humorous graphics. In the following interview, I ask her some questions pertaining to both freelancing and designing juvenile cards (also see Figure 8-10).

Ron. How did you become a card designer?

Judy. Well, I went to Garland Junior College. I received an associates degree in graphics, and from there I did my fieldwork at Rust Craft for three weeks. They offered me a job while I was there, so that I would have a job when I graduated.

Ron. At Rust Craft, you painted cute, humorous designs. How did you get started in that?

Judy. The first year I was there, they more or less tried you at everything, and each artist worked with an art director. The art director I had was a floral artist and tried to get me to lean towards being a floral artist, which I really wasn't that comfortable with. I always wanted to do the fun, child-oriented cards. So after a year of trying everything, I just decided I felt more comfortable doing the children's line of work.

Figure 8-10
By Judy Mitchell. A small gift card with a quiet sentiment.
Courtesy of C.R. Gibson Co., Norwalk, Conn.

Ron. Where do you get your ideas for doing cutes? Do you rely on any one area?

Judy. Probably right out of my head from things that I see related to children, or what kids are doing, or what they're playing with . . .

Ron. Just from observation?

Judy. Yes, and just from things in my past that I remembered and things that seemed funny and cute to me. You use a lot of other greeting cards for reference ideas or what the greeting card industry thinks a cute teddy bear should look like . . . squash the features down and no belly buttons, and I suppose that after you've done one cute teddy bear, you've done them all. After you've learned the basics of what makes something cute, then you're more or less on your own to develop your own situations.

Ron. How long did it take to develop your own style?

Judy. It took about three years. Your own personality always comes through in your work, and if you are off the wall, then your stuff will always be off the wall. It's how you see the world that comes out in your work.

Ron. Do you like freelancing?

Judy. I love it. I love it because you can make your own hours. You can take a vacation when you want to. If you don't feel like working one day, you don't have to work. There's a lot of work out there from what I can see, and it's just a question of how much you want to do. You can work a twenty-hour week. You can work a sixty-hour week, if you know what the companies are looking for. You know, if they want it sky blue, make it sky blue. I mean, that's what they're looking for, so do it the way they want it.

Ron. So you're able to compromise without too much trouble?

Judy. No problem. . . . I've never told anybody, "No, I can't do this assignment." I've always done every assignment. Once you get established in the greeting card business as a freelancer, it's not hard. I mean, the first years you have to go and scrounge around to find work and keep making contacts. It takes a long time to get your name around and build a reputation with a company so that they'll call you and you don't have to keep banging at their door.

Ron. So, you are basically going to stay within the field?

Judy. Forever. Until my arms drop off. I'm very happy doing just what I'm doing. I don't get frustrated thinking why I'm not more famous. I'm very content. I enjoy seeing my things in print.

Ron. Lastly, do you have any tips for people starting out in freelancing?

Judy. I would strongly suggest working for a company as a full-time artist, if possible. You have to learn the ropes. You have to learn the basics. . . . There's an awful lot that you cannot learn through the mail, and you'll waste a lot of time sending things out and having them come back. Because there are certain rules, like no belly buttons, that you learn by doing. It's very important to work in the field before you can freelance. You just can't pick up a brush and paint a greeting card and send it out and hope to sell it.

Chapter Nine

Related Paper Products

Figure 9-1 *Holly Hobbie Dolls* by Judy Mitchell. Courtesy of the artist, American Greetings, and GORHAM, DIVISION OF TEXTRON, INC., Providence, R.I. (licensee).

In retrospect, the 1950s and early 1960s were prosperous times. By the mid-1950s, some of the larger greeting card manufacturers found they had outgrown their production facilities. This induced them to build new and larger plants. It was also a good time to think about the future.

Almost simultaneously, several companies began to diversify by placing more emphasis on the creation of card-related paper products. New machinery and equipment were added as the new plants were built.

The vision of the 1950s had been correct.

The companies that began making paper products soon discovered new and larger markets. In a sense, one thing led to another. The paper products field is still expanding at an impressive rate. Companies such as Recycled Papers, that began in the 1970s, quickly turned to producing related products. Today, nearly all card publishers make some related products, either directly or indirectly. The larger companies are interested in a wide variety of products. They are constantly testing for new markets. In this area, American Greetings is a leader. American Greetings has made a concerted effort to come up with new ideas and new products, as the following profile details.

Profile:
American Greetings
and Those Characters from Cleveland

Note: Much of the following information has been supplied by Mr. Morry Weiss, President and Chief Operating Officer at American Greetings. It is with his cooperation and that of American Greetings that this profile is presented.

American Greetings is not only one of the world's largest and most successful companies, but it is also one of the most creative companies as well. American Greetings started out as the horse-drawn business of Jacob Sapirstein in Cleveland in 1906. In 1918,

Figure 9-2
Holly Hobbie. With the great success of Holly Hobbie, Strawberry Shortcake, and Ziggy, American Greetings is continually expanding its horizons. Copyright 1981, American Greetings Corp. 35B488-6E

Irwin I. Stone became the company's second employee, out of necessity. He was nine years old at the time. In the past seventy-five years, some aspects of the company seem not to have changed much: the company is still located in Cleveland, and Mr. Stone is still an integral part of its success, although he is now the chairman of the board and chief executive officer. American Greetings has made some substantial changes, however; from the two-person business of 1918, it has grown into the world's largest publicly-owned manufacturer of greeting cards and related products, employing almost 17,000 people in twenty-four plants throughout the world. American Greetings produces over 1.5 million cards each year, which translates into a total revenue of nearly $600 million.

American Greetings has long been recognized for the creative role it has played in the card industry. The popularity of Holly Hobbie products (see Figure 9-1) and the great Ziggy cartoon designs have brought the company many awards, but more recently, there has been an even greater success story—that of Strawberry Shortcake. These three creations have proved so enormously successful that American Greetings has set up a new division, called Those Characters from Cleveland, to handle these products and those yet to come. The future of this division is promising: Strawberry Shortcake merchandise totalled $100 million in its first year alone, and in 1981, retail sales generated almost $500 million. Strawberry Shortcake is presently licensed to over fifty companies and appears on over 300 products, ranging from wallpaper and sleeping bags to dolls, toys, and children's clothing. In short, Strawberry Shortcake has become a household word for anyone with children or grandchildren.

American Greetings is staffed with over 400 in-house artists and writers, who produce nearly 12,000 original designs yearly. Little freelance work is given out, although the company will always look at a new and creative design. How else could it have gotten this far?

GIFT WRAPS

Some paper products are more closely related to cards than others. With the exception of the repeat, designing and producing a gift wrap is very similar to card-making.

Gift wraps are repeated designs created to appeal visually, whether seen in part or in whole. In this respect, they differ from other repeated products, that is, wallpaper and tile design.

To make a gift wrap, the artist starts out by designing an original motif called a *repeat*. Repeats vary in size from 4″ to 16″, standard sizes being 9″ × 9″, 9″ × 11″, and 11″ × 11″. The majority of wraps I have done have been 11″ × 11″.

There are two common types of repeats: the straight repeat and the locking repeat.

Straight Repeats

All wraps are repeated several times to create the final product. The actual number depends upon the size of the original design. There are some wraps that repeat only twice, but a more common figure would be eight or more.

The easiest repeat to lay out is termed a *straight repeat*. This involves an original design with straight edges, either square or rectangular. The final design is created by placing duplicates of the original repeat around the original. Such repeats are generally easy to spot. In fact, they are meant to be seen. The pattern created by repetition is a vital part of the concept.

In a straight wrap with an original repeat of 4″ × 4″ and an overall dimension of 20″ × 24″, the original would be reproduced thirty times per sheet.

All straight repeats require careful and accurate measurements. The wrap shown in Figure 9-3 is a partial straight repeat[1] with a built-in safeguard against error. This particular wrap was done with markers, not one of the most accurate media to work with. I was concerned the horizontal bands, between the ducks, fish, and so on, might not line up evenly when repeated. The solution was to break up those bands into a series of dots and dashes, alternating on each side. That way, every repeat would line up when a dot and dash came together. If the bands were solid, any error on my part or the printer's would have been easily noticed.

Locking Repeats

Locking repeats are also called *lock-in repeats* by some. There may also be other terms used to describe this type of wrap, but the basics remain the same. An original design is created with

---

[1] This wrap is actually a locking repeat along the vertical edges and a repeat along the top and bottom edges.

Figure 9-3
This wrap by Ron Lister was done with markers and is a combination of a straight repeat along the top and bottom edges and a locking repeat along the right and left vertical edges. Used by permission of Norcross-Rust Craft Divisions of Windsor Communications Group, Inc.

slightly irregular dimensions. Instead of straight edges, the design elements may protrude out from an imaginary straight line (locking repeats still begin with square or rectangular dimensions). However, any time a part of the design does advance out from the straight edge, it must recede inward at some point on the opposite side of the original for the design to lock together. Locking repeats fit together like giant pieces of a puzzle (see Figure 9-4).

The basic function of such repeats is to disguise the duplications as much as possible. The viewer should have to search to find the repeat.

Note: Locking repeats may protrude up to two inches from the straight edge, but seldom more. Most commonly, such repeat patterns protrude about an inch.

Figure 9-5 shows an original wrap of poppies. The colors (orange, blue, and green) were precepted. The object was to design the middle portions of the original repeat first, working my way out toward the edges. Note, even in these central areas, there is an uneven use of positive and negative space. This is important. Some of the leaves and flowers touch, while others do not, leaving various amounts of negative space

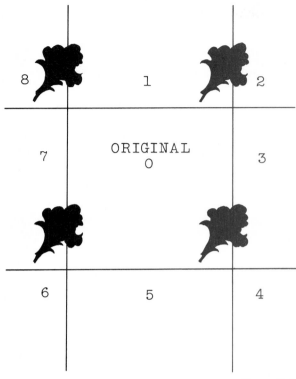

Figure 9-4
Making a locking repeat. This diagram shows where a single design element (in black) appears when the original design (o) is repeated (1-8).

in the interior. There is a reason for this. When the outer edges of the original are later lined up with the duplicate repeats, it is impossible to line up each leaf on a flower perfectly. It would take extraordinary accuracy to have them all touching yet not overlapping each other. This is certainly not the type of thing printers like to try. Instead, the wrap was designed to allow only a few places to touch. In this way, some of the negative spaces in the outer areas would be open and uneven. If done properly, this simulates the same type of positive-negative areas found in the central areas of the original repeat and makes it difficult to spot the repeat when the wrap is reproduced to its final size.

There are other considerations as well. In all types of wraps, it is important to leave enough of a bleed around the perimeter of the original. In a straight repeat, a simple $1/8''$ or $1/4''$ will usually suffice, but locking repeats are more involved. Some companies allow parts of the design to protrude as much as $2''$ from the basic format. If this is done and a colored background has been used, then the background bleed must be sufficient to cover all the repeats. When in doubt, always check with your art director. It is better to leave too much of a bleed than too little.

Figure 9-5
Poppy Wrap by Ron Lister. Note how the top and right side perimeter of this wrap lock into the bottom and left side perimeters. Used by permission of Norcross-Rust Craft Divisions of Windsor Communications Group, Inc.

Designing a locking repeat is usually time-consuming. It is necessary on all wraps to use a grid overlay for measuring the correct edges. Most locking wraps are laid out by using moveable strips of tracing paper. As each edge of the original repeat is drawn, it is traced onto one of the strips. The strip is then placed in every position where a duplicate repeat will eventually line up with the original. This is shown in Figure 9-4. In this way, all eight corners of the original can be visualized, and all necessary corrections can be made.

Other Considerations

Most locking repeats are designed without a definite top and bottom. These wraps require placing the design elements at different angles or in various positions to allow viewing from any direction.

Also, some art directors do not like the components of a wrap to be too large, the idea being that even a small package should display most of the repeat. Other art directors are not in the least concerned about such things. I had to redo a wrap once for this reason, and have never forgotten it. So, always ask when in doubt.

CALENDARS

After several thousand years, calendars have recently become big business, at least from our vantage point. Calendars are being marketed in ever-increasing numbers. Even without precise statistics, it is fair to say the calendar market is just about flooded. The major card companies now plan their new calendars two and sometimes three years in advance. So, if you are interested in this area, you had better plan ahead.

Figure 9-6
Rabbits by Ann Boyajian. Each page of this calendar was machine stitched over fabric. Used by permission of Norcross-Rust Craft Divisions of Windsor Communications Group, Inc.

The variety of calendars has also grown tenfold in the last decade. This is one market where fine arts, cartooning, photography, and just about every form of illustration are shown together on the same rack. Sizes now vary with equal impressiveness. There are small desk calendars, standard hanging calendars, and giant poster calendars. Still, getting the opportunity to do a calendar, or even a part of one, is difficult. Calendars are a major undertaking for publishers, and each one is given considerable attention.

I have my own special interest in calendars. For the past few years, I have been trying to promote my fine arts commercially. I have had several oil paintings published in calendars (see Figure 7-9), and I am presently trying to sell my pastels. Figure 9-6 displays a beautiful fine arts-oriented calendar, designed by Ann Boyajian. Each design was machine-stitched onto fabric. The grace and dexterity of the stitchery is quite beautiful. In this case, thirteen individual designs were submitted and approved.

In summation, calendars are selling well, but the number of opportunities for artists remains relatively small. Recently, I was informed by two of the major card companies that fine arts calendars are not selling very well. One company told me they are producing fine arts only to have them on the racks, just to say they have them in their line.

The high visibility of calendars between October and February is also deceiving. It is still a market that competes less than half of the year. But for all of this, calendars are still an attractive package and a chance to do something special.

STATIONERY

Stationery comprises a surprisingly finite field. Most card companies do put out various types of stationery, from note cards and writing pads to boxed sets, but the numbers are small. In addition, stationery is one of the more conservative aspects of the card industry. The function of writing materials is the primary concern of most publishers. Richly designed stationery may be found, but not in abundance. For freelance artists, this means most publishers have little trouble assigning such work to their in-house staff or to their favorite freelancers. There simply is not a large demand for freelancing in this area. However, if you are interested, contact card companies or stationery companies like Eaton and show them suitable designs. Do not show cards and expect to be assigned stationery. If you want to design stationery, then do so, and send in actual samples, whether originals or printed.

Note: Different formats such as fold 'n' send or envelope cards are assigned on specifications given by the individual companies. Templates or written specifications should be provided to you.

Figure 9-7
Fold 'n' Send Stationery by Ron Lister. Here, the stationery and envelope are incorporated together. *Specs* for such products are supplied by the company. Courtesy of Red Farm Studio.

STAMP

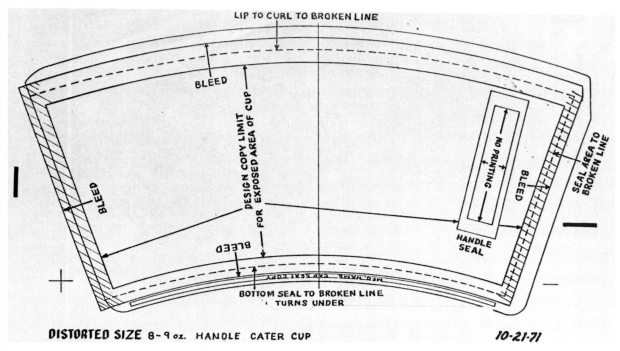

Figure 9-8

An eight ounce paper cup template. Templates are often used to explain more complicated specifications. This one shows the dimensions of the cup as well as which areas can be painted.

PARTY GOODS

This comprises a wide assortment of paper products that are often overlooked, especially considering the large role they have played in the card industry for so many years. A partial list of goods includes table covers, placemats, paper plates and cups, napkins, and a variety of party favors.

There is little need to worry about how a napkin or paper cup is designed for production. Exact specifications are supplied by the company. Figure 9-8 shows a paper cup template. All the necessary information has been provided on it, including where the artwork should be placed.

Because of the special dimensions involved in party goods production, companies normally have their in-house staff design them. Of course, there are exceptions if you are willing to look them, but I would not count on making a living from party goods sales.

OTHER PAPER PRODUCTS

In addition to cards, stationery and wrappings, there are dozens of closely related paper products: gift enclosures, invitations, announcements, recipe cards, place mats, book plates, book markers, posters, bags, packaging, puzzles, and a large assortment of party goods. All of these particular items are manufactured or at least handled by greeting card publishers. In addition, there are many more products designed on paper but produced in other materials. Each year the number of all types of related products increases. Availability, too, has dramatically changed. Today, a good card store offers much more than just cards. A variety of paper goods and boutique items is now commonplace.

As an example, a look at Hallmark stores provides an insight into the direction now being taken by the major card companies. Hallmark has expanded its market in several directions. First, it is noticeable how much space is devoted to paper goods other than cards. Many of these are new or relatively new products.

For example, while decals and stickers are not exactly new items, their popularity and visibility are. Hallmark has a complete line of products available. Their "Super Seals" include many types of popular subjects and graphic designs. The line also includes nationally popular characters such as the Muppets, Smurfs, and Garfield the Cat. There are foil stickers and glittered stickers as well. The seals can be purchased in small packages or singly off rolls. All things considered, there is little one cannot buy in the way of decals and stickers.

Hallmark also sells a wide range of other products from baby photo albums to figurines. Sometimes other companies are contracted to do the work and Hallmark handles the finished product. For instance, jigsaw puzzles by Springbok are directly related to Hallmark.

Most card companies are expanding their product lines to include a wider variety of both juvenile and adult gift items. As mentioned, American Greetings has licensed "Strawberry Shortcake" to appear on over 300 different products!

All of this reveals the potential of paper products that the major card publishers discovered long ago. But how does this affect us as designers? From a freelance point of view, the effect is marginal. There are quite a few product manufacturers who give out freelance work, but you must first seek them out. In general, it is likely you will run across more assignments as a full-time employee. The more specialized the product, the more likely it will be assigned to an in-house artist or a trusted freelance designer. However, there is a considerable amount of work to be found in designing the more basic types of paper products such as gift wrap and party goods. Also, it is worth noting that all of these products are first created on paper and that working in any of these areas is little different from card designing in general. Naturally, each product has its own function, which must be considered in the design. However, with specifications and a working dialogue with the art director, creating such products should not be alien to a card designer.

Unfortunately, many people still think there is a trick to getting into other areas of designing. My advice is simple: Look for what you would like to be doing yourself. When you find it, design a small portfolio based on what you see. Submit your work to the appropriate companies, and see what happens. Remember, the closer your portfolio work resembles the type of job you are seeking, the more seriously your work will be taken.

You may have noticed in the list of other paper products a variety of small card-type items: recipe cards, gift cards, and the like. There appears to be an increasing market for concepts where full-color and multiple pages may not be necessary. I believe these areas are worth investigating, especially if you are thinking about producing your own cards. If you have an idea, why not try it out? Test it, and see what happens.

Figure 9-9
A Bridal shower gift card. Though often smaller, gift cards are essentially like all other greeting cards. Courtesy of Hallmark Cards, Inc.

Figure 9-10
Judy Mitchell. Bookplate. There are many ways of becoming involved in paper designing. This bookplate design was submitted by the artist in an open competition held by the library. Courtesy of the artist.

Figure 9-11
Sandra Boynton. *I never met a carbohydrate I didn't like.* Ceramic cup box. Though the caption and art work appear together on the box, they are separated on the actual cup. Courtesy of Recycled Paper Products.

This is often the only thing separating those who are producing and those who are not. You have to try first.

PRODUCTS DESIGNED ON PAPER

Like the previous category, this includes a large number of products associated with the general card field, but with the difference that these products are translated or transferred to materials other than paper once they are designed. In the past, this area of gift and boutique items was quite separate from the general card market, but now an increasing number of related products are being sold along with cards. This means more card designers are getting involved with new products.

Basically, there are two ways in which nonpaper gift products tie in with cards. First, there are a number of products already related to the general sentiment-gift market. This includes ceramic and porcelain figurines, dolls, plates, cups, beer steins, and so on. This market has expanded tremendously in the past decade, with much of the interest from the major card companies. For example, card shops now offer a variety of ceramic cups, from personalized name cups to floral designs and antique automobiles. Figure 9-11 shows a humorous cup design created by Sandra Boynton. It is relatively easy to adapt such artwork for a cup. Only the limitations of size and proportion differ here from a standard card design.

This leads to a second consideration. Many nationally recognized cartoon characters have found their way onto a variety of products. You can now buy designer clothes for your Snoopy doll, bumper stickers with Garfield the Cat, Smurf watches, and just about Strawberry Shortcake anything!

In some cases, the card company or the actual creator of the product handles all the design requirements personally. More often, characters such as Strawberry Shortcake or Holly Hobbie are licensed out to other companies to be redesigned as new products. Figures 9-1 and 9-12 show artist Judy Mitchell's recreation of the Holly Hobbie characters as fine porcelain and cloth

Figure 9-12
Judy Mitchell. Four "Holly Hobbie" dolls, © 1983. American Greetings Corp. (licenser) and GORHAM DIVISION OF TEXTRON INC., (licensee). Providence, R.I.,

dolls for Gorham Textron, Inc. It was through her previous association with Gorham that Mitchell was awarded the contract to redesign the characters. When designing the dolls, she needed to show each one from a variety of angles (viewpoints). These are referred to as *elevation drawings* and are necessary for creating the die stamps and tools for production.

It took a great deal of coordination between Holly (the original designer), American Greetings (the licenser), Gorham Textron, Inc. (the licensee), and Judy Mitchell (the new designer) to create this beautiful set of dolls. The dolls average approximately fifteen inches in height and cost over $100 each, making them one of the more costly card-related gift items. Because of the high degree of quality control necessary to produce such a valued product, freelance assignments of this sort are not given out without serious consideration. Only proven artists can expect to land such large accounts. Still, the general point is that the opportunities are there, and card designers are involved.

If you wish to become involved with any particular line of products, write to the company. Inquire into portfolio requirements and work availability. Consider each product and each company individually. Steer your artwork in that direction. You must be able to prove you can handle the job. If you have a cartoon character or graphic style you believe would look good as a specialized product, it is up to you to convince the manufacturer. Unless a particular card style relates directly to a product, do not expect to interest anyone by simply showing card samples. When artist Michael DiGiorgio first contacted the Danbury Mint about designing wildlife illustrations for their ceramic plates, he sent samples of his wildlife illustrations instead of his card designs. He has since painted several plates for them. In all cases, give the art director a good idea of how your artwork can be used as a specific product. Remember, if you need exact specifications, ask for them. Most art directors are willing to help.

RELATED CHRISTMAS PRODUCTS

The healthy expansion of Christmas products is itself indicative of the current trends in the business. The Christmas line of products dominates the year for most card companies. In turn, this provides work nearly year-round for card artists. As mentioned, some companies such as Sidney J. Burgoyne & Sons in Philadelphia or CPS Industries in Franklin Tennessee devote most of their efforts towards Christmas cards, or, in the case of CPS, wrappings. Besides cards and wraps, there are scores of other Christmas paper products including: fold 'n' send notes, post notes, gift tags, place mats, invitations, and a wide variety of packaging concepts and label designs. Nonpaper items include candles, ornaments, wall decor, table settings and party favors.

Specialized Christmas products are a growing concern, and the card companies are nearly always in need of new designs and fresh ideas. Sometimes, in fact, they even get desperate. An example of the latest in Christmas card concepts is a tree card that actually lights up when opened. These are being marketed by George Good, through Alfred Maizer, Inc.

Note: Specialized Valentine's Day products (including almost anything with a heart on it) are growing in demand. It seems likely this area is destined to continue to expand for years to come. Where will the next trend take us? Figure that out, and it could be worth a great deal.

WALLPAPERS

Designing wallpaper is similar to gift wrap designing in that repeats are used. Precepted colors are also common. However, wallpaper colors are hand-separated. It is considered second-rate to do otherwise. Also, wallpaper repeats vary a good deal more than gift wraps. For instance, Morton Jonap Ltd. uses basic divisions of 36″ repeats, including 18″ and 9″ on down to 1″ units.

If you are interested in wallpaper design, see as much of it as possible. Make notes on what subjects are currently being marketed. Intense colors, dramatic subjects, and foils and leafs are currently popular. Go to local dealers and look through their sample books. Find patterns and subjects which appeal to you, and try to paint a few variations. You can adapt what you see, but try to send the right samples to the right companies. Most art directors prefer to see painted samples or sketches. Slides and prints are not as welcome. Remember, too, these companies often have a small in-house staff and favorite freelance

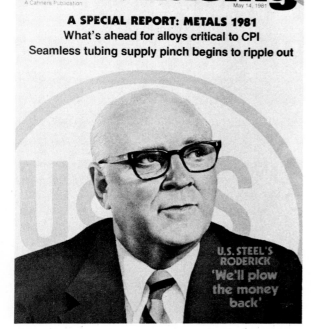

CPI EDITION

Purchasing

A Cahners Publication

Chemarkets
Ethanol tags are steady 6

May 14, 1981

A SPECIAL REPORT: METALS 1981
What's ahead for alloys critical to CPI
Seamless tubing supply pinch begins to ripple out

U.S. STEEL'S RODERICK
'We'll plow the money back'

Figure 9-13
By Anatoly Dverin. A pastel portrait for *Purchasing* magazine. Once a successful card designer, Dverin is now an established illustrator. Though these two fields (card designing and illustration) appear to have similarities, they actually do not overlap very much. Courtesy of *Purchasing* magazine, a Cahners Publication.

contacts who do the majority of the designing. To break in, your work will have to be well-presented and somewhat original.

Note: Here are a few more tips on submitting wallpaper designs. As mentioned, companies prefer to see painted sketches. Wallpaper sketches are large, full-scale drawings which show the overall design. However, because each company works with different-sized repeats, your repeats do not have to be completely worked out. Save that until you know the exact size of the repeat and you have a contract to finish the job. Also, try to avoid any elements in the design which are angular or lead the eye in any type of diagonal motion. Any repeat which creates descending or ascending eye movement will not be acceptable.

MAGAZINE AND BOOK ILLUSTRATION

These two areas are basically separate industries and are quite removed from the conventional card business. Book and magazine publishers have little or no direct connection with card publishers, except that quite a few card designers have become illustrators. In truth, there has been a lot of mobility between the card and illustration fields. My long-time friend Anatoly Dverin, who is profiled in the last chapter, is one example of this. Once a very successful card designer, he is now a successful magazine illustrator and has illustrated quite a few books as well. That profile and most of the last chapter discusses moving on to other fields. For now, I would like to point out one important factor. If you are interested in becoming an illustrator, approach it with intensity. Be sure to give the field its due respect, and *never* submit greeting cards to help land an illustration job. They are separate fields; treat them as such.

Working and Selling

Figure 10-0 *Graphic Tulip* by Ron Lister. Used by permission of Norcross-Rust Craft Divisions of Windsor Communications Group, Inc.

Chapter Ten

Freelancing

Figure 10-1 By Ron Lister. Detail of Geese card.

THE ADVANTAGES OF FREELANCING

Working on your own as a freelance artist can be fun, exciting, and profitable. It can also be frustrating and insecure; and at times, it can be all of these things in short succession. Patience and diligence are as important as mastery of the more technical aspects of the business.

There are many advantages in freelancing. To begin with, the forty-hour week becomes obsolete. Of course, you may find yourself working the occasional sixty- or eighty-hour week, but they are *your* hours. When I first began to freelance on a full-time basis, I was greatly surprised to find out how much work could be done within the old forty-hour framework. When painting from 9 a.m. to 5 p.m., it was necessary to pace myself; but on my own, it became possible to work in short, intense spurts and still accomplish whatever was called for. For one thing, it is easier to concentrate on painting when there are no outside distractions, and in an art studio, there are many distractions. Combined, these factors greatly enhance not only how much work can be done, but also, how much free time becomes available, time to develop new contacts or new interests. In my own case, I found time to develop my fine arts and get into teaching, music, and eventually writing; but, it was the freelance work that supported me while I ventured into these other areas. Now when I return to painting a card, I am refreshed. Freelancing is never stale or boring.

Besides being a part-time or full-time career, freelancing is also a business. It is a great way to learn the ins and outs of self-employment. You can learn about bookkeeping, tax breaks, and the countless other facets involved in working on your own. All of this helps you to rely more on yourself. It makes you better professionally by becoming more involved in all areas of the card field, not just painting.

THE DISADVANTAGES OF FREELANCING

I have few complaints overall about freelancing, but those few should be detailed.

My basic frustration has always concerned how to control the work flow. Sometimes it is necessary to work a twelve-hour day, while other days are nearly static. During the first two years I freelanced, I cannot remember taking more than a three-day vacation at any one time. It is always difficult to find a time when everything falls into place and a week or two opens up.

Another concern is keeping an emotional balance. Nobody likes to have a job rejected, but occasionally it happens. It is natural to be concerned when something does not work out and to see that the situation is corrected. At the same time, it is necessary to look ahead and not be slowed down because of a failure. What often complicates these matters is being alone. Much of the time, being alone is a plus factor, but in times of emotional stress, it can magnify problems. It is not easy to keep confidence when alone; self-doubt has a nasty habit of creeping in. Because of this, I recommend seeking out professional friends for support. We all go through bad times. Try not to go it alone.

Figure 10-2
By Tom Cante (signed Plato). Used by permission of Norcross-Rust Craft Divisions of Windsor Communications Group, Inc.

Profile:
Michael DiGiorgio,
Freelance Wildlife and Card Artist

Michael DiGiorgio is a freelance artist currently working in Potsdam, New York. He has a fine arts background and has worked full-time as a card designer. Michael is primarily interested in easel painting. His specialty is wildlife art, and his paintings have appeared in numerous publications. Because Michael has been freelancing full-time for a relatively short period (two years), I asked several related questions about his new career (see Figures 10-3 and 2-7).

Ron. How did you go about setting up as a freelance artist?

Michael. I first took slides of my best paintings and greeting cards. I then went out to stores that sold cards, books, calendars, and the like which had the

Figure 10-3
A personal stationery and business card design by Michael DiGiorgio. Courtesy of the artist.

look and feel that I could do. I wrote to these companies and sent my slides and a resume, although your work speaks for itself.

Ron. How long has it taken to establish yourself?

Michael. As far as I'm concerned, I'm still not established. I am still having to worry about my future. I am much better off than I was two years ago, but I have a long way to go.

Ron. How many companies do you currently work for?

Michael. Currently, about twenty companies, with a majority of my work coming from about five or six. The rest trickle in now and then.

Ron. Is this enough? How many companies do you think one should work for?

Michael. I feel I never have enough. There may be a reason why a company will no longer need your service, be it short or long term. This is when you need other options. I am constantly sending out for work. I like to play it safe. On the other hand, one should be careful not to go overboard and get too many assignments at once.

Ron. What do you like the most about freelancing?

Michael. I enjoy being able to build up my future on my own. I also like having the ability to live anywhere I wish and still have work. For example, I now live in Potsdam, New York. It is a small community which has virtually no work, but it is a beautiful little northern New York town and I love it here.

Ron. What do you find most distasteful about your job?

Michael. The problems with freelancing are serious enough to break many beginners. Not everybody is meant to do such work. We are apt to take rejections and criticism personally. The longer you are in the business, the better you are able to handle it.

Rush jobs are frustrating, but are unavoidable. You also learn about "express" mail and U.P.S. Also, dealing with inconsiderate companies is the worst part of my business. A majority of those I deal with are very good, but I do run into a bad one now and then.

Ron. What is your goal?

Michael. My goal as an artist is to eventually be able to support myself as an easel painter. I am very happy to do commercial art, but it could never equal painting to my own specifications.

I would like to dispel the theory that anyone who

chooses to portray native or, more specifically, wildlife in their paintings is merely an illustrator.

Ron. Do you have any advice for newcomers to the freelance market?

Michael. Ah, yes, advice to someone starting out. I feel like I am starting out, and I regularly seek advice. I have gotten direction from many sources, be they artists or not.

First of all, find out what you are good at and work from there. Find shortcuts . . . to speed up your working time. Don't be afraid of rejections, but never let a job leave your board until you are satisfied with it. . . . Learn about making a presentation of your work.

FINDING THE MARKET

The freelance market is very extensive and has been expanding steadily over the past several years. Access to that market is easier than ever, but accessibility has also made the field more competitive. If you can find it, so can others. The general card market consists of a few very large card publishers and numerous smaller ones. The two largest companies, Hallmark and American Greetings, buy very little freelance art. They both have large in-house art staffs and give what little freelance art there is to former employees. This is all the more painful if we con-

Figure 10-4
Horse painted with acrylics by Anatoly Dverin. Used by permission of Norcross-Rust Craft Divisions of Windsor Communications Group, Inc.

sider that perhaps eight out of every ten cards sold in the United States is produced by one of these two manufacturers.[1] Looking at this from another direction, however, we can see just how big the greeting card industry must be to support so many other publishers and all of us as well.

It is those few remaining larger companies that can provide us with the most work, companies like Gibson and Recycled. For instance, Recycled buys upwards of a thousand illustrations a year. Besides this, nearly all the smaller card companies rely on freelance art to fill out their lines. Quite a few use freelance art exclusively.

With the competition being as tough as it is, I believe it is necessary to approach freelancing with some initial planning. This requires some footwork. Research your local area. Find out where the different companies are selling their products. Learn to recognize different companies by sight, and single out those you like. At some point, you will have to assess your own work in relation to what you see on the market. Friends may help, but only *you* can determine if you are ready to compete or not. As a guide, compare your designs directly with similar types of art on the shelves. Once you feel your work is as good as what you see, then submit it.

During this time, it is helpful to start collecting reference, other cards, and especially, names and addresses.

Publications

The most widely used publication is *The Artist's Market*, an annual hardback published by Writer's Digest Books (9933 Alliance Road, Cincinnati, Ohio 45242). This book is printed on thin newsprint and contains approximately 500 pages. There are 3,000 markets listed in advertising, art studios, book and magazine publishing, newspapers, record companies, and art publishing. About twenty-five pages are given to the greeting card industry. *The Artist's Market* lists companies, art directors, addresses, and telephone numbers. It reports individually on contract requirements and company needs. Money is also discussed. There is an introductory chap-

ter giving general information on the art profession: presentation, portfolios, and so on.

The Artist's Market can be purchased in most local bookstores and art supply stores. It is updated and reissued every year.

It is worth remembering that *The Artist's Market*, good as it may be, is not all-inclusive. There are companies that, for various reasons, are not listed in this guide. If you find a company you like and it is not listed, here are a couple of things you can do. First, check the back of the card; if there is an address, or even part of one, write it down. Later, you can call Information and get a telephone number. In just two calls, you can usually reach the company. Most art directors do not mind explaining their policies about freelancing over the telephone. Of course, you can write instead of calling, but I recommend direct contact whenever possible. If there is no address or even city listed on the back of the card, then ask to speak to the store's card buyer. Sometimes this is the manager, but often it is not. Explain your problem, and they can usually supply an address.

The National Association of Greeting Card Publishers and Gift Wrappings and Tyings also publishes the free *Artists and Writers Market List*. It can be obtained by sending a stamped, self-addressed envelope to 600 Pennsylvania Avenue, S.E., #300, Washington, D.C. 20003. This pamphlet is small, but does contain a few dozen listings. Of special interest are the listings for verse writers.

There are also several standard directories listing card publishers. If an address is all you need, you can try one of the following directories found at most libraries.

1. *Standard Directory of Advertisers*, an annual listing of 17,000 corporations, published by the National Registrar Publishing Co., Inc., 5201 Old Orchard Road, Skokie, Illinois 60077. (Card publishers are listed under Publishers, Printers, Engravers, and the like.)

2. *Standard & Poor's Register of Corporations, Directors & Executives.* An annual three-volume directory, published by Standard & Poor's Corporation, 25 Broadway, New York, New York 10004.

3. *The National Directory of Addresses and Telephone Numbers.* This book is published

---

[1] This number is impossible to verify, but according to several sources, it is probably a fair estimate.

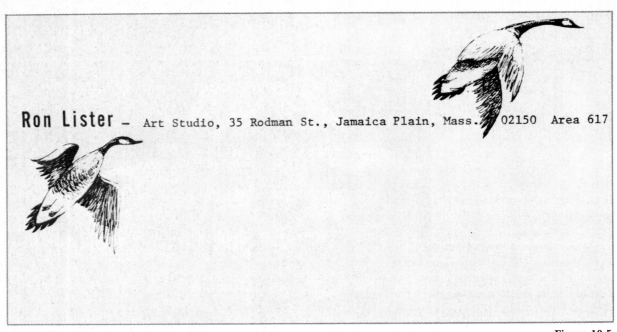

Figure 10-5
Personal stationery (detail) by Ron Lister. Having good stationery and business cards helps to make a good first impression with companies.

4/2/85

every two or three years by W.C.C. Directories Inc., 850 3rd Avenue, New York, New York, 10022.

For those interested in keeping up with trends in the market and the occasional address or contact, there is *Greetings Magazine*. This publication is deemed a must by many freelance artists and individual card producers because it lists new products, upcoming trade shows, and an overview of the entire market, coast to coast. The annual subscription rate is only $10.00 ($20.00 in Canada) and the magazine is published monthly by MacKay Publishing Corp., ~~95 Madison Avenue,~~ New York, New York 10016, telephone (212) 679-6677. 309 5th Ave ny ny 10016

GETTING STARTED

Queries

First contacts with a publisher should be kept simple and direct. If a query letter is sent, it should not contain anything that does not bear directly on the business at hand. Art directors are too busy to handle much more. If you know a company accepts freelance work, then your first letter might as well include samples.

Usually, a query letter includes a few pertinent facts about yourself and any inquiries you have about the availability of work. If the entire letter is two short paragraphs, fine. Avoid being

wordy or confusing. Ask only basic questions. If your work is accepted, the publisher will furnish you with any necessary information.

Expect any return correspondence to be short and to the point. A letter of acceptance is likely to be as short and as impersonal as one of refusal, so do not be shocked.

Note: Be sure that in making first-time contacts that all queries and/or portfolios are sent with a self-addressed, stamped envelope included to ensure return delivery.

Resumes

There are a few publishers that ask directly for resumes; most do not. Art directors have a marginal interest in such information. They are more concerned with seeing your samples. My advice is that a resume is not necessary unless asked for. If one is sent or delivered, it should be concise, clear, and short. There are various opinions on how long a resume should be, but in freelancing, a two- or three-page biography is not required.

Letters of Refusal

Being turned down is a fact of life within this business. Learn from it when it happens, but do not let it slow you down. If a letter of refusal states why your work was not accepted, there is sometimes the possibility of submitting another portfolio in the future, once the original problems have been resolved. If they like your second portfolio, they will likely forget your original one.

Some refusals are more permanent than others. If a publisher tells you they like your work but cannot use it at the present, then there is still hope. If they tell you that you will be contacted in a couple of months or when something is available, do not count on it. Intentions are often different from reality. For instance, if I am told I will be contacted in August when the new line opens, I will plan on taking the initiative. Just prior to August, *I* will contact the company and remind *them* of their verbal agreement.

If, on the other hand, I am told my cards will be kept on file, but no later date of any sort is mentioned, I will try to read between the lines. If I really want to work for this company, I may contact them again anyway.

Persistence is one tool we can and must use. Pursue all avenues. Remember, too, companies frequently take on new art directors. From reviewing back issues of *The Artist's Market*, it appears that some companies have a new art director every year. This can work to our advantage. An incoming director may appreciate our work more than the previous one. Of course, the reverse can also be true.

Portfolios

The best remedy for being refused at one company is to be accepted at another. By sending out several queries or portfolios at a time, the chances of your work falling into the right hands greatly increases. It is not a particularly sound idea to have only one portfolio, no matter how good it is. When I am trying to find work, I keep at least one or two portfolios in the mail with an extra one at home, ready to go if needed.

When interviewing in person, it is nice to show a leather-bound portfolio, but when sending through the mail, it is considerably better to have a more portable system. Expenses are high enough as they are.

In any case, portfolios sent to greeting card companies should include primarily greeting cards. Printed cards, proof sheets, or photocopied work is best. Originals should remain at home unless specifically asked for. Your samples should display a talent and ability to do different types of subjects, but do not send card styles to companies that do not print those styles.

There are a few publishers who do prefer to see original art in the form of finished cards or rough sketches. H. George Caspari, Inc., and Evergreen Press are two such companies. Sending a portfolio of originals or printed samples from which an art director can directly purchase

Figure 10-6
By Ron Lister. When sending in a portfolio, try to keep the format uniform. Do not send photos, cards, and slides all together. Used by permission of Norcross-Rust Craft Divisions of Windsor Communications Group, Inc.

work is called a *stock portfolio*. This has been previously discussed in the section on photography. The principle is the same. In stockpiling, the artwork is intended for actual sale. Generally, it is the smaller card companies that buy artwork from stock portfolios. The larger publishers normally view portfolios to see what type of work they may assign to you. This differs only when you have artwork that is unique. If your work is truly different, then you might submit it for direct purchase to any company, large or small.

Note: Be careful not to send two or more samples of the same design out for sale at the same time. It could be embarrassing if two publishers agree to buy it simultaneously.

How Many Samples?

There is no written law concerning required numbers. I follow the generally accepted practice of sending small portfolios (under twenty samples). If necessary, more can always be sent, but never feel bound to a specific number, any number. Present only your very best work, even if it means displaying only a handful of samples. Remember, numbers do not impress; quality does.

It should also be noted that many art directors prefer loose samples to bound portfolios. They like to be able to handle the cards directly and to see them singly. Each sample should be labeled on the back with your name, address, and phone number, in case of separation.

Note: When sending out samples, it is best to stick to the same format. Try to send cards or prints that are roughly the same size. Do not send large prints, smaller cards, and even smaller slides together.

Finally, remember to show designs fitting a company's "look" as closely as possible. Samples you know look different are a waste of time.

Portfolio Protection

Most portfolios are handled indirectly. The artist is not present with the showing. It is common to question whether your work is safe in the hands of others, and some artists do not like a company to keep their work on file. Having the art copyrighted is one form of protection, but can be expensive and time-consuming (copyright laws are discussed later in Chapter Thirteen). For now, let me say that nearly all card publishers are honest about these matters. There are some solid reasons why your work is safe. The basic one is simple. Any company that steals a design will gain a reputation in a very short time. It simply is not worth it to them. However, if you feel your art needs to be protected, if you have designed a cartoon character or have developed a unique style or technique, then by all means copyright.

Portfolios also need protection in physical terms as well. There is always a risk when sending packages through the mail. I believe very

Figure 10-7
When sending in portfolios, the general rule is quality not quantity. Send only your very best work. Courtesy of Hallmark Cards, Inc.

few portfolios are actually lost, but even one, if it is yours, can be tough. Portfolios are more often damaged by improper packaging. I used to insure all my mail to the limit, but the cost of doing this has risen dramatically in the past few years. Presently, I do not insure most of what I send. Instead, I put extra effort into the packaging. This is a subjective decision based on the fact I have never had a portfolio lost. But such decisions must be made individually.

Agents

An *agent* is a second party who arranges sales and provides contacts. This person becomes a representative of the artist and is paid a commission on each work sold, by agreement. A good agent may take twenty-five percent or more. When you move into the highest levels of the art and illustration fields, an agent frequently receives forty or fifty percent of each commission. To the newcomer, this may seem extraordinarily high, but then so are the fees paid out at the higher levels of the business. A good agent can accomplish several important things. First, he or she can allow the artist time to concentrate on the art instead of having to go out and get more work. Secondly, a good agent can line up commissions we would not be able to get on our own. Finally, a good agent can command higher fees for commissions and directly raise our market value.

My advice is not to worry about agents. When your workload becomes too heavy or when you are ready to branch out into new areas, then get an agent. By then, it is likely an agent will have contacted you.

As a final note, some designers have agents all over the country. How many agents are required will be dictated entirely by your individual circumstances. For more on this subject, see Chapter Thirteen.

Contracts and Royalties

There are two basic contracts to consider: the first is an *artist-agent* contract and the second, a *company contract*. The principal aim of any agreement is to ensure both parties clearly understand their responsibilities. If you are about to sign an artist-agent agreement, I suggest two things. Make certain *all* areas of concern have been adequately covered, and be sure the contract includes a clause permitting periodic review of the artist to agent payment for commissions. For more on contracts, I recommend *How to Sell Your Artwork* by Milton K. Berlye (Prentice-Hall, Inc., Englewood Cliffs, N.J., copyright 1973).

Written company contracts are not as standard as they once were, but some of the major publishers still use them. At Gibson, artists are often given a three-month trial contract. If all goes well, then yearly contracts may follow. Each contract should stipulate, for the company, the responsibility of the artist to do the work and get it in on time. For the artist, it should insure a certain amount of work, monthly or yearly, and should also provide other basic protections: fees, royalties, and the like.

It is worth remembering even a written contract does not provide total security. Contracts can be broken fairly easily, though, in most cases, nonrenewal of a contract is the usual method of discontinuing one's services. On the positive side, there are designers who have worked under contract for twenty-five years or more to a single company.

Royalties are even less prevalent than contracts. Only those artists with substantial reputations and talents are generally in a position to bargain. There are, however, a few companies that give royalties to their artists.

If you are interested in receiving a royalty, you may have to fight to get one; but in the end, it will likely be worth it.

The Pay Scale

Payment for freelance artwork varies a good deal. If you are new to the market or simply do conventional cards, you will probably have to settle for less. Surprisingly, there are a few companies still offering to pay under $100 for a full-color art. These companies represent the lowest end of the scale and should be avoided if possible. Of course, it is important to get something—anything—printed, so these companies still find needy artists to do the work.

The average pay scale for conventional cards falls between $125 and $300 per card. Some publishers pay above this from the start, but generally, it is necessary to build up a reputation first.

Top card designers can get two to three times

those prices listed, but, again, the higher up the scale, the lower the number of artists involved.

Gift wraps pay approximately twice as much as cards, and special jobs usually bring higher fees. Designing a ceramic plate can bring $1,000 or more.

At the highest end of the scale, artists can make really big money. A few names and statistics might astonish some people. With royalties, hard work, and a good publisher, the limits are still being defined.

FREELANCE WRITING

Writing gags and verse for cards is just as competitive as the visual end of the business. The major complaint of the card companies concerns originality. Much of the writing submitted for sale is simply old hat. Either it has been done many times over, or it is out of date. Some themes remain eternally useful—love, hope, sympathy, and so on—provided the designer can find a new way to present it.

The best way to break into the market is to be current. Go out and see what is being done now. Look closely at how different situations apply to different sentiments. In all attempts, be specific. Give your writing direction. Aim at a specific occasion or event. Remember, cards are event-oriented. If your writing cannot service a definite occasion, it is probably of no use.

There are two broad classifications in writing. The first involves serious sentiments, like those found in conventional and inspirational cards. The second concerns the lighter side of the market, from gentle-humored cute and humorous cards to the more outrageous studio designs.

Humorous and Studio Cards

Humorous cards are conventional in shape (format) and general concept. Verse, sometimes prose, is used to complement the illustration. These cards generally convey a gentle humor, not the punch of a studio gag line. Figure 7-12 displays a Z-folded humorous card designed by Ray Medici (see his profile in Chapter Seven). The close relationship between the drawing and verse is standard in both humorous and studio lines. Each element is designed to complement

Figure 10-8
By Mike Rodgers. "Life is funny . . . By the time you know the answers . . . (inside) They change the questions!" Studio cards are long and tall in format, and the writing generally relies on a gag line. Used by permission of Norcross-Rust Craft Divisions of Windsor Communications Group, Inc.

the other, while neither is intended to stand on its own. As a general comparison to this, the rest of the conventional card lines do not have this close verse-to-illustration relationship. The tie-in is more basic, and often, the verse and caption make no direct mention of the subject.

Humorous and studio cards are closely related. The artist who paints one type often does the other as well.

Studio cards are long and rectangular in format. This distinguishes them visually from conventional cards, and, in fact, most studio cards are displayed on separate racks. The writing comes in the form of gags or short prose with a punch line. Gags are often irreverent or irreligious, but not always so. Gag writers must be aware of contemporary trends, and, like humorous writers, they must also be able to visualize the concept as a whole.

Submitting for Humorous and Studio Cards

Submitting writing for the studio and humorous lines is slightly different than for conventional ones. Ideas should be neatly printed or typed on a folded *dummy* or mock-up of the card. Try to use the same size and shape dummy as would appear in the final design. If the card is a studio design, then use a long, single-folded piece of paper. Place the gag and punch line approximately where it might go in the final design.

Many writers also include a rough sketch to accompany their gags. Some are quite good at cartooning and submit the whole card (design and gags) as a unit. This certainly helps to sell the concept, but is not an absolute necessity. It is also possible to print the message on a 4″ × 6″ or 3″ × 5″ index or file card. Each sample should have an identification number, name, and address on the back.

Written messages are submitted in batches of ten to fifteen gags or verses. As with any type of portfolio, send only your best work. Research this carefully. If you send any out-of-date material, the art director may not even finish reading through all of your samples.

Conventional Writing

This category labeled "conventional" covers a lot of ground. Most cards are considered conventional and use a sentimental verse or one-line

Figure 10-9
By Sandra Boynton. "In honor of Your Birthday (inside) a 21 Bun Salute." In any type of writing, it is very important not to lose sight of the occasion or function of the card. Courtesy of Recycled Paper Products, Inc.

prose to convey the message. Subcategories include juvenile cards (under 12), everyday cards (birthdays and the like), special occasion cards, and inspirational cards (religious). Writing for these lines does not require the same visual-to-verse relationship as in studio cards. But it is necessary to have a good understanding of the occasion/function for which you are writing. Whatever type of message you wish to convey, remember who buys the cards as well as who the cards are intended for.

Figure 10-10
By Ron Lister. In conventional writing, the relationship
between the verse and the art
is often minimal.

Submitting Conventional Writing

All work should be printed or typed on 3″ × 5″ or 4″ × 6″ slips of paper, or index or file cards. Be sure to include an identification number, name, and address on the back of each message. When submitting for seasonal or occasional cards, be sure to allow the necessary eight to ten months advance time.

Finding the Writer's Market

The National Association of Greeting Card Publishers puts out a free pamphlet on finding the writer's market (see "Artist's and Writer's Mar-

ket List" under "Publications"). They also have a membership roster available to writers by sending a written request to the same address: 600 Pennsylvania Avenue, S.E., #300, Washington, D.C. 20003.

The *Writer's Market*, an annual publication of Writer's Digest, Cincinnati, Ohio, is the most useful market directory for card writers. It lists the general book and consumer market in detail. It also devotes numerous pages to gag writing and more to greeting card companies specifically. The *Artist's Market*, also published by Writer's Digest, *does not* list companies' needs relating to verse. A somewhat different list of card publishers appears in the *Writer's Market*.

The *L.M.P.* (Literary Marketplace/Directory of American Book Publishing) covers thousands of book publishers, book clubs, magazines, and the like. It is an annual directory put out by R. R. Bowker Company of New York and London. This publication can be found in most libraries and is a good source for names and addresses but not necessarily for greeting card companies specifically.

THE BUSINESS END OF FREELANCING

Making a Good Impression

Freelancing is a business venture as much as it is an artistic one. All aspects of the business should be handled professionally. When contacting someone about work, it is worth having good stationery for the occasion. My stationery includes my name, address, and telephone number, plus a simple graphic design (see Figure 10-6). Business cards and self-promotional materials should likewise reflect your direct intentions along with the necessary personal information. Anatoly Dverin's self-promotional illustration (Figure 10-11) plays up his keen drawing abilities. His name is artistically designed on the page, while the other printed information is kept to a minimum visually. In the years I have known Anatoly, I have seen quite a few of his self-promotional illustrations. Each one has been designed for a specific market or clientele. This is one business where keeping a high profile pays off.

Anatoly Dverin
Illustrator

9 Oak Drive
Plainville, MA 02762
(617) 695-2931

Anatoly

Figure 10-11
A self-promotional flyer by An-atoly Dverin. As a commercial artist, it pays to keep a high profile. Courtesy of the artist.

Taxes and Freelancing

How you pay your taxes depends on how much freelancing you do and how much of your income it accounts for. If freelancing amounts to any major portion of your yearly wages, then it is probably worth filling the long tax return forms and itemizing everything. Contact your local government center for the necessary forms and any pamphlets pertaining to self-employment. Be forewarned, there are quite a few. Following this procedure, you file an estimated tax return quarterly, money included. At year end, either a final check or a return will even things out. Though very few people are audited each year, it is still necessary to document all items which relate to the business. I find this part a great annoyance. Keeping old receipts, bills, invoices, and so on is time-consuming. However, my accountant assures me it is necessary. It is surprising how many things actually do relate to the business; and, if documented, they can all be deducted from your taxes. For instance, if you rent a five-room apartment and convert one room into a studio, then twenty percent of all related bills can be deducted. This includes oil, gas, electric, telephone, and, most important, rent. Likewise, car maintenance and mileage, and travel and food expenses can be deducted if they relate to the business in any reasonable way. So start saving your receipts and documenting your business. Credit cards are quite useful this way.

If your state has an arts and humanities foundation or your city has an arts council, then be sure to contact them. Find out what they can do for you. In Massachusetts, the Arts and Humanities Foundation publishes a pamphlet called "Taking Care of Business." It lists courses and workshops on a variety of subjects. They also offer counseling, referrals, tax advice, and legal advice.

As a final note, a good accountant and/or tax consultant can be a great aid. See if you can find someone to help out. It may even be possible to exchange services to keep costs down. Perhaps you could design a logo or business card in exchange for having your taxes computed.

Chapter Eleven
Working Full-Time

Figure 11-1 Copyright by Wallace Tripp. (inside) "Olive You!"
Courtesy of Pawprints, Inc., Jaffrey, N.H.

Not many artists envision working full-time as a card illustrator. It was the last thing on my mind when I graduated from college. But, in retrospect, my five and a half years as full-time board artist are a valued experience. I met many talented people and learned a great deal about the commercial art field as a whole.

In some respects, working full-time was also a safe way to break into the business. It allowed me the time to learn the basics, gain confidence, and develop my painting skills, while being paid. It also exposed me to a variety of experiences not found on the outside. I personally believe the advantages of starting out as a full-time board artist outweigh any disadvantages.

GETTING HIRED

It is a common misconception that you must be a proven card designer *before* a publisher will hire you. Certainly experience helps, but art directors are always on the lookout for new talent, people who are willing to learn. There are several practical reasons for this. First, if you can

A Greeting on Father's Day
'For 'You,
SON

Figure 11-2
Horses by Jay Doucette. This card shows an illustrator's touch. In fact, many card designers do go into illustration. Used by permission of Norcross-Rust Craft Divisions of Windsor Communications Group, Inc.

draw well and know a little about color, you might be a good risk. An art staff can teach a new artist about greeting card color, layout, and subject without too much difficulty. It is done all the time. Each company has its own look, and it is unreasonable to think that new artists, even with previous experience, will pick up on that look immediately. In most companies, three to six months are reserved to adapt and develop. In some cases, up to a year is allowed for developing into a consistent performer.

Another reason why inexperienced artists are hired is related to the overall mobility of de-

signers and illustrators. Accomplished card designers often go into freelancing or on to other illustrative fields. Others become assistant art directors or take on management positions. Of course, there are experienced artists who remain on the board, but the turnover in the card industry is fairly high and new positions are periodically available.

There is yet another reason for bringing in new talent—money. An inexperienced designer will always make less than an experienced one. To some companies, this is an important factor. To others, it means little or nothing.

Interviews

First impressions are very important. When interviewing, be neat and professional in appearance. Dress casually, but try not to look sloppy. Act professional. Try not to appear nervous or overly nonchalant. Be aggressive, but not cocky. When asked questions, answer them as directly and concisely as possible.

It is not necessary to be funny or amusing. Let your work speak for you, and perhaps most important, *never* apologize for anything in your portfolio. That only brings attention to things best left alone.

At a large company, you will often first be interviewed by someone other than the creative director or art director. Artists are often screened by an assistant or a personnel employee. I used to screen portfolios myself. My instructions were to set up another appointment if I thought the art was substantial, or to advise the artist what should be corrected before applying again. Sometimes it took several visits before an artist got to see the creative director. Do not be shocked if, after all of this, the director appears only to glance at your portfolio. This is somewhat common.

If invited back for another interview, then go back, no matter what you think your chances are. At Rust Craft, there was a woman who interviewed numerous times over the better part of a year. She kept working and adding to her portfolio and was eventually hired. I recall this story because of an ironic twist. It took nearly a year for this artist to finally land the job of her dreams. She had been very persistent. Yet after working for about six months, she quit. Designing cards was simply not what she had expected.

Sorry about your accident

Figure 11-3
Raccoons by Nancy Kellerman.
Courtesy of Red Farm Studio

Profile:
Nancy Kellerman, Card Designer

Nancy Kellerman has worked as a full-time board artist at four different card companies. She is presently freelancing while raising a family.

Ron. Tell us about your background in art.

Nancy. My education in art was not much. I spent two years at the Dayton Art Institute. I did learn some things, but most of what I've learned has been by working. Art schools just don't teach you anything about how to deal with a full-time job. They don't press the fact that you should make things neat and clean and square and reproducible.

Ron. How did you first decide to go into greeting cards?

Nancy. I didn't decide to go into greeting cards. I was looking for a job in Cincinnati, Ohio. As a last stop, I remembered somebody had told me there was a card company there called Gibson Cards. So, on my

way out of town, at 4:15 in the afternoon, I stopped by Gibson, and they hired me on the spot. I had never done cards in my life.

Ron. How long did you stay at Gibson?

Nancy. About three and a half years. Because I had lots of black and white experience, they put me in this area where I did color separations. They were still doing hand separations at the time. So, for a year, I did that. It was really a good education. Later on, I did studio cards.

Ron. You've worked for several card companies. Can you cite any major differences between them?

Nancy. Well, Gibson Cards was a very professional place. I worked there in the middle 1960s, and everything was well-run and well-organized. They didn't bug you if you took a lot of time, and nobody came around and hung over your shoulder. At Rust Craft, they wanted to get the stuff out quick, and we hardly had any supplies to work with. Another place I worked was Charmcraft. I was the assistant art director for nine months, but left because it was so disorganized. This was about 1970. I've heard that the ownership and everything has changed, so I really don't know what the deal is now.

Ron. And you worked for Red Farm?

Nancy. Yes, they did very good reproduction and got very good results. There was a lot of leeway for the artists, although they wanted to have a certain look, which was the Red Farm look; my style fit very well with that kind of look.

Ron. Your style is quite tight, close rendering and lots of detail. Where did that start?

Nancy. That's the way I've always drawn. I always liked a lot of detail in everything I did.

Ron. So you didn't learn that from any one company?

Nancy. No, that's me, but I did work for five years for the telephone company, doing tons of speedball lettering for the Yellow Pages. Indirectly, everything you do helps, I guess.

Ron. What advantages are there to working full-time, now that you've worked as a freelance artist for several years?

Nancy. Well, aside from the weekly paycheck, I like the companionship of working with other artists. The isolation of working at home by yourself is not very conducive to creativity. Just being around other artists is stimulating, and I miss that.

Ron. Do you plan to work full-time again?

Nancy. Probably, when the kids get bigger.

Ron. What advice would you give for anyone starting out?

Nancy. I would say go around and look at greeting cards. Study the market; study what the styles are. Just look at what other people are doing. Try to keep

Figure 11-4
By Sandra Boynton. Courtesy of Recycled Paper Products.

largest card manufacturer in the world, with approximately 1,200 staff employees. Of these, over 100 had art-related jobs.

Each company with a large staff has its own system, but, for the majority, the basic methods of production are remarkably similar. Even smaller companies operate on similar lines with the exception that, because of their smaller staff, more functions are performed by each individual.

CREATION OF A CARD

Phase One

New cards are essentially born on the old display racks. It is part of a sales representative's job to report back to the company on which cards are selling. They do this by keeping tabs on card numbers each time they replenish the display racks. Back at the office, it is the line planners, also called product planners, who are respon-

up-to-date. . . . Try to keep up with the media, not just in cards, but in every way. Subscribe to a lot of magazines, and build up a clippings file. That's really important. You have to have reference. 'Cause nobody can make up that stuff. There's nobody who can know exactly what a poinsettia looks like. Also collect greeting cards. You really have to know the market. Lastly, you have to be able to draw. In greeting cards, you have to be fairly specific about what things look like. It's a fairly conservative market, and if they (public and companies) want an old car, it's got to look like an old car.

CARD PRODUCTION

Whether you ever work as in-house artist or not, it is still helpful to understand the basic mechanics of how a publisher produces greeting cards. There are often dozens of people who actually work with, and on, the cards we design. Quite a few of these people have an input even before we get the assignment. The following is a general outline on card production based on my experience with Rust Craft Publishers. At the time I was there and gave tours through the various departments, Rust Craft was the third

Figure 11-5
By Ron Lister. Most cards start in the office of a *Line Planner*. Used by permission of Norcross-Rust Craft Divisions of Windsor Communications Group, Inc.

sible for developing the new card lines. This involves various types of market research. From sales representatives, they learn which cards are doing well. They subscribe to numerous magazines and trade publications and round out their research by keeping up with what is selling for other companies. This is done by going out to the various card shops. With all of this outside information and a certain amount of input from within the company, they can begin to plan the next card lines.

At periodic meetings, the creative director and upper management meet with the line planners to consider any broad changes in company policy and to plan, in detail, the upcoming card lines. All card lines, whether seasonal or monthly, are put into a working order. In a large company, each line planner's duty may involve a very specific portion of the card line. For the Christmas line, for instance, he or she may be responsible for just floral designs. Working with a prescribed budget, the line planner divides the new line up into an exact number of new cards

and reissued cards termed rehashes. Each card is considered according to cost, so the line planner must know about printing and finishing costs. In the end, an exact number of designs are fit into the line. The object of all of this planning is to insure a full range of choices for the consumer without unnecessary duplication.

Now the planner can start collecting leads (reference). Leads are intended to give the artist a point of direction from which to start. They can indicate a particular format, layout, color scheme, or technique. Some jobs include several leads, others none at all. Leads can come from cards, books, magazines, almost anywhere; it depends on how much of a guideline the line planner believes an artist needs to fill the order precisely. *Note*: Smaller companies tend to be less precise about this because there is less of a chance of duplication.

Finally, a specification sheet or spec sheet (see Figure 11-6) is written out on each design. This may be an envelope with leads, caption, and verse included inside or a separate page attached

Figure 11-6
A *Specification Sheet* gives the artist all the technical requirements on a design.

CORPORATE DESIGN SPECIFICATIONS	LINE: RLVT 1-80 LINE

CORPORATE DESIGN NUMBER	TYPE FOLD	COMMON SIZE FOLDED	COMMON SIZE OPEN	PRINTING PROCESS

DESIGN REQUIREMENTS:

UNITED STATES	UNITED KINGDOM	CANADA	PRICE / TITLE / TIES / QUANTITY
PLANNER	PLANNER	PLANNER	UNITED STATES (A) REPL.# 40A 487x-7 45.0
SIZE OPEN	SIZE OPEN	SIZE OPEN	40AF 4878-2V Hello
SIZE FOLDED	SIZE FOLDED	SIZE FOLDED	UNITED STATES (B) REPL.# 40BG 3594-8 35.0
EMBOSS	EMBOSS	EMBOSS	40BG 3557-2 Tribute
GOLD BRONZE	GOLD BRONZE	GOLD BRONZE	UNITED KINGDOM (A)
DIE-CUT	DIE-CUT	DIE-CUT	35 2510 B'day General
LEAF	LEAF	LEAF	UNITED KINGDOM (B)
GLITTER	GLITTER	GLITTER	
BAKE	BAKE	BAKE	UNITED KINGDOM (C)
FLOCK	FLOCK	FLOCK	
ATTACHMENT	ATTACHMENT	ATTACHMENT	CANADA (A)
INSERT	INSERT	INSERT	
INSIDE SPOT	INSIDE SPOT	INSIDE SPOT	CANADA (B)
STOCK	STOCK	STOCK	
FORM	FORM	FORM	CANADA (C)
BACK-UP	BACK-UP	BACK-UP	
SEE REVERSE SIDE ☐	SEE REVERSE SIDE ☐	SEE REVERSE SIDE ☐	

Figure 11-7
By Marge Pendleton. Cards may be reviewed by a review board, but it is ultimately the art director who has the final say. Courtesy of Red Farm Studio.

to the leads. The specs are then passed out to the various art directors, and phase two begins.

Phase Two

Large companies usually have their artists divided into groups. There may be a room(s) for those who paint florals, cutes, figures, and so on. Studio cards are designed by a separate department. Each room may be further divided into cubicles with movable wall dividers. An art director or assistant art director is assigned to each group and is responsible for giving out assignments. Less experienced artists are watched over more closely and are assigned specific jobs. They are also required to check back more frequently on their progress. In my last years at Rust Craft, I worked in a room that handled a variety of subjects. We were allowed to choose much of our own work. It was only when we got to the bottom of the barrel that the art director was forced to assign the last few unwanted assignments.

Each company has its own system for assigning work, but generally, experience acquires a certain amount of freedom.

After the assignment is received, the artist paints the card (see Chapter Four). When fin-

ished, it is first shown to the immediate person in charge. If approved, the card is then reviewed with other cards at a weekly or biweekly *design review*. Reviews are judged by any number of people: assistant art directors, line planners, board artists, even factory workers; but it is the creative director who has the final say.

One of several things can come out of a design review. The card may be rejected outright, in which case it is thrown out and the specs are either returned to the original artist or to a different artist. Sometimes, however, the card is returned to the line planner to have the specs altered. This indicates faulty planning and in a way vindicates the artist.

The remainder of designs in review are accepted. Some are approved as they are, without corrections, but often a minor change or fix is required. Almost all fixes are done by the artist who designed the card.

After the card is accepted, the artist's input is generally over with.

Phase Three

Finished designs are photocopied and a dummy or *working comp* is made. This mock-up shows how the card will function and where each component (artwork, inside spot, caption, and so on) will go. Next, the card is split up temporarily into those component parts. The title caption and verse (which are typed on paper at this stage) are sent to the lettering department. There, the proper typeface will be chosen, and any necessary calligraphy will be painted. *Note*: Calligraphy is nearly extinct in the card industry. The once-prominent position of the hand-letterer has largely been replaced by machines.

While the lettering goes one way, the artwork goes another—to the reproduction department. In the repro room, each design is measured and registered, and all finishes are translated into black and white. If a card has blind emboss on it, the reproduction department will redo the embossing to show the printer how to make the dye stamp. Most finishes are shown in black ink on prepared acetate overlays, while blind embossing (see Chapter Six) is shown with pencil on a film overlay.

Reproduction artists are required to be neat and precise. They are responsible for making sure the card will fit together when all the separate components are rematched in the final product.

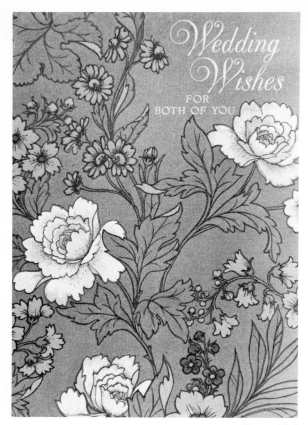

Figure 11-8
Wedding Wishes. The newer *graphic* look of the seventies replaced the *painterly* styles of the sixties. The dark blue background *was also an innovation at the time.* Courtesy of Hallmark Cards, Inc.

At some point, either before or after the artwork has gone to the repro room, it must also go to the printer to be photographed and color separated (see Chapter Twelve). From this, proof sheets or tear sheets are checked over by the art directors and the printer for color corrections and blemishes, termed *scum marks.* A good publisher will review the proofs two or three times, if needed, to make certain the final printing will be clean and accurate.

In the end, the card is printed. Lettering and finishes are added, and it is folded, packaged, and boxed. Later, the cards are trucked to the stores for sale. This whole process takes eight to ten months to complete, though it can be done in much less time for special rush jobs.

Finally, let's take a look at what it is like to work at the largest of all card companies, Hallmark.

Profile:
The Hallmark Approach

As the undisputed leader of the social expression industry, Hallmark represents the very center of the traditional card industry. Annual sales are estimated at more than a billion dollars. With such overwhelming success, it is interesting to note that the average person knows very little about Hallmark beyond its slogan, "When you care enough to send the very best." Few people are even aware that the name Hallmark incorporates the family name of Hall. Founded by Joyce Hall in 1910, they are still a privately-owned corporation and are still located in Kansas City.

I wish to present three key factors I believe account for Hallmark's great success over the years. First, Hallmark understands its buying market extremely well. Indeed, they have created much of it themselves through years of advertising and specialized sales. The Hall of Fame television specials were introduced back in the 1950s. In the 1960s, the first Hallmark card shops were opened. Prime-time television advertising began in the 1970s, and today Hallmark is diversifying its sales program to include more three-dimensional products. There are now more than 20,000 stores carrying Hallmark products, of which about 7,000 are independently-owned specialty shops displaying the Hallmark name. Their salespeople also know that as much as eighty-six percent of Hallmark's clientele are women, and the shops cater to many specialized needs.

A second factor in the Hallmark story has been its conservative approach to the business as a whole. Hallmark has never shifted its interests away from the card field as so many others have done. They have always concentrated their efforts on producing top-quality card products. That quality has never been in doubt and has certainly led to greater sales (and indirectly back to a conservative approach). Hallmark is respected as it is; to change for the sake of change has never been considered.

The third key to Hallmark's success has been the company's respect for, and care of, its 14,000 employees, which includes a creative staff of 600. Hallmark has always sought to attract young and new talent out to Kansas City, rather than spreading its base. To do this, they offer an attractive package that is much more than just a job. About half of the company's employees work in Crown Center, which is a $500 million complex. It is situated on eighty-five acres and features a 730-room hotel, a second 750-room hotel, two office developments, and an indoor shopping mall with fifty retail stores and twelve restaurants. The company also sponsors national art competitions and exhibitions, trips, and many extras.

Above all, respect and creative freedom give the artists at Hallmark the opportunity to work at their best.

Chapter Twelve

Printing Your Own Cards

Figure 12-1   A linocut by Ron Lister.

Most of the problems involved in making your own cards are cost-related. It is hard to keep overhead expenses down and still produce a competitive product. Printing in volume is the best method of lowering printing expenses, but selling in volume can be difficult. Either way, these concerns make private enterprise a perplexing task. Producing your own cards takes confidence and initiative as well as an outlay of capital. This is not a job for the faint of heart. However, success, if it comes, is all the more satisfying.

Printing cards in large numbers does reduce expenses substantially, but exactly how much depends upon several variables, including what type and method of printing is used. Each printing process dictates a different set of expenses, and each printer offers a certain number of options based on what type of press he or she operates. Because of this, it will be necessary to make your own comparisons and evaluations.

PRINTING PROCESSES

There are four primary methods of commercial printing:

1. *Letterpress* (printing from a raised surface)

2. *Offset-Lithography* (printing from a flat surface)

3. *Gravure* (printing from a depressed surface)

4. *Silkscreen* (printing through a mesh screen)

Whether you plan to print in color or black or white, on a glossy or matte finish, or in large or small numbers are all factors that will determine your choice of printing. As we will see, each method is quite different.

Letterpress

Letterpress is the oldest form of printing. It comes from the art of woodcutting, in which nonprinting areas are cut out of a wood block leaving a relief surface. This raised surface is inked, and the ink is transferred to the paper under pressure. In today's commercial printing, the relief printing surface, called the plate, is normally a lightweight plastic or chrome-covered surface, though metal plates are still common as well. The actual relief is made by *photoengraving* (see "Photoengraving").

The pressure used to transfer the ink from the plate to the paper is supplied by the printing press. The presses can be divided into three general classes: platen, flat-bed, and rotary. A platen press has two flat surfaces, a bed with the printing plate and a platen, which supports the paper. The bed and platen open and close much like a trouser presser (or a clam). Platen presses are usually sheet-fed (individually) and print a single color onto most any type of stock, thick or thin. It can also be used for embossing, die-cutting, and scoring.

Flat-bed cylinder presses have the paper stock wrapped around a revolving cylinder. The plate is attached to a flat bed which moves back and forth. Under pressure, the revolving cylinder and the moving bed produce the printed sheet. The press is usually sheet-fed. There are both one- and two-color models.

The rotary press has two rotating cylinders, a plate cylinder and an impression cylinder. The relief plate is semi-cylindrical and is molded from the original plate. The plate is locked on the plate cylinder, and the paper stock is fed between the two rotating cylinders. Rotary presses can be sheet-fed or web-fed (a roll of paper that is cut after printing). Models range from one-color to six-color. They are accurate and fast, and are used for large runs such as newspapers, magazines, and packaging.

Note: Generally, good quality letterpress printing requires the use of smooth, coated papers. These coated stocks are relatively nonabsorbent, which helps to keep the inked surface even and uniform. More absorbent papers can be used by making the surface of the impression cylinder more resilient.

Photo-Offset Lithography

This is the most common method found today for printing greeting cards, gift wrapping, business cards, posters, labels, books, newspapers, and magazines. There are several labels for this process: lithography, offset, photo-offset, offset lithography, and photo-offset lithography. They all refer to the same process, which can most technically be termed *planography*. Planography means printing from a flat surface. It is based on the principle that oil and water do not mix.

Offset printing can be very complicated, but basically it is a three-cylinder press: a plate cylinder (holding the cylindrical printing plate), a rubber-blanketed offset cylinder, and the impression cylinder. The thin printing plate is prepared for printing by two sets of rollers. One set inks the plate; the other wets it. Water is retained only on the nonprinting areas, and the ink is retained only on the printing areas. The plate and offset cylinders are then rotated against each other, and the printed areas are transferred onto the rubber blanket, which covers the offset cylinder. This transferred image is now a mirror image of the original and is thus backwards. The

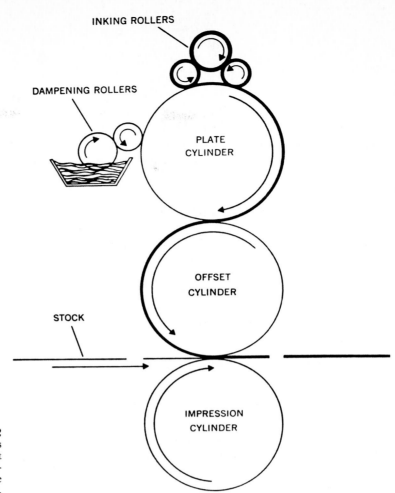

INKING ROLLERS

DAMPENING ROLLERS

PLATE CYLINDER

OFFSET CYLINDER

STOCK

IMPRESSION CYLINDER

Figure 12-2
Offset-Lithography. The term "offset" refers to the use of an extra printing cylinder that takes the reversed image from the plate cylinder and corrects it as it is transferred to the paper stock.

final step involves contact between the offset cylinder and the impression cylinder, with the paper stock passed between the two. The corrected image is then transferred by pressure onto the paper as it is fed through. The final print is once again a duplicate of the original.

Offset presses come in many sizes and models, from one-color, sheet-fed presses to very large multi-colored, web-fed models.

Note: There are several good books on offset printing. Recommended is *Photo-Offset Lithography* by Z. A. Prust (published by the Goodheart-Willcox Company, Inc., South Holland, Illinois, 1977). This book covers everything from careers in offset printing and graphic art to photo conversion and binding. Of course, it fully covers the offset process as well.

Gravure (Intaglio) Printing

Gravure comes from the art of engraving or etching (intaglio) in which the artist uses an etching tool or acid to incise the lines to be printed. Ink is forced into the lines, and the nonprinting surface is cleaned off. Under great pressure, pa-

per and plate are brought together. The ink is then lifted out of the plate onto the paper.

Commercially, all gravure printing is done on a rotogravure press. As with offset lithography, the printing plate is wrapped around one cylinder called the plate cylinder. This cylinder then revolves in a pool of ink. A doctor blade immediately wipes the surface clean, leaving ink only in the incised lines of the printing plate. The paper then comes between the printing and impression cylinders, and the pressure pulls out the ink by suction onto the paper stock.

Gravure is capable of producing rich, deep tones because of the density of the ink used. It can print on a variety of surfaces, both smooth and textured. Rotary presses are nearly all web fed and high speed. Some are 150 inches wide. They are used for packaging and printing on foil and cellophane. They can also be used for artwork, catalogs, and pamphlets.

Silkscreen

This process is perhaps the most versatile of all. It is capable of printing on almost any surface: paper, board, glass, plastic, metal, or fabric.

Figure 12-3
Six small silkscreened cards by Emily Hall. Copyright by and courtesy of the artist, Jamaica Plain, Mass.

The printing plate is really a finely meshed screen, stretched very tightly over a wood or metal frame. The screen can be made of nylon or silk or of metals, in some cases. Nonprinting areas are blocked out on the screen with a stencil, which is either cut out, painted on by hand, or photographically prepared. The stencil is placed directly on the screen. The frame with the screen facing down is then placed on the surface to be printed. Ink is poured onto the screen and forced through the mesh by a rubber squeegee onto the printing surface.

One great advantage here is the ink can be very dense—much thicker than other printing processes will allow. The results can be striking. Brilliant, opaque colors can be applied to a variety of surfaces, and even lighter colors can be printed over darker ones.

Most silkscreening is done by hand, although there are automatic presses. It is a messy and smelly process requiring plenty of room and fresh air. Silkscreening is not recommended for pregnant women.

With a minimum of tools, silkscreening can be done by anyone. Recommended reading is *Silkscreening* by Maria Termini (Prentice-Hall, Inc., Englewood Cliffs, New Jersey, 1978). This is a comprehensive guide to the process, with many good illustrations.

Photoengraving

Platemaking is broken into two categories: line and continuous or gradated tone. Designs having no gradations in tone are formed by solid black lines, dots, or flat areas. This includes pen and ink, brush drawings, or any medium which produces solid areas of black. For these types of design, a line plate can be made. For any drawing or painting which has gradated tones, a halftone plate must be made. Line plates and halftone plates can also be combined. Of the two, line plates are the least expensive to make.

Making Line Plates

Here the artwork is set up and photographed using film which is insensitive to values of gray. It registers only black, and only solid areas are developed. The rest become nonprinting areas.

The film negative is then taken out of the camera and turned over so that the original image will be duplicated when printed. The negative is then placed on a plate glass, called a flat. The flat is placed down on a metal or plastic

134

plate which has been coated with a light-sensitive chemical. An exposure is made using arc lamps, which project light through the transparent portions of the negative. The plate is then fixed to let the areas that have been exposed to light acid-resistant. These areas then become the printed image.

The plate is then given several acid baths which eat away the unprotected portions and leave the treated lines or solid areas in a raised or relief position.

Halftone Plates

For any artwork with gradated tones (shadows, modeling, and the like), a halftone plate must be made. In order to simulate modulating tones or values, it is first necessary to break the photographic image into a series of tiny black dots. These dots vary in size, but even the largest are quite small to the naked eye. When viewed from even a short distance, they blend together and are perceived as continuous tones.

The dots themselves are created by the addition of a halftone screen in the camera. This screen is made up of two sheets of glass, each with etched lines equally spaced. The lines are both parallel and opaque. The two sheets of glass are cemented together, allowing the lines to cross at right angles. A coarse screen may have only 50 lines to the inch. A fine screen may have as many as 200 lines per inch.

Note: The type of screen used is determined by the amount of detail found in the artwork. A very highly detailed design may require a fine-lined screen, with as many as 200 lines per inch, but screens this fine cannot be used on rough paper stocks. Thus, newspapers, which are printed on rough newsprint stock, use a halftone screen of 50 to 70 lines per inch. A sophisticated magazine, however, may use screens as fine as 200 lines per inch because they print on a very smooth, glossy coated paper.

The basic difference between line and continuous tone platemaking is the use of the half-

Figure 12-4
This enlarged photo shows a *half-tone image* at very close range.

tone screen. The artwork is simply photographed through the screen which breaks the picture up into dots. The treatment of the film is otherwise similar to line plates. Any picture taken through a halftone screen will be broken into dots throughout the entire surface. Even areas of the original artwork that were pure white will now have pinpoint dots in the negative. This is called a square halftone. In a square halftone, there are no pure areas of absolute white. To obtain pure white, the dots in those areas must be removed or dropped out. This is called a *highlight halftone*.

COLOR SEPARATION AND COLOR CORRECTION

Three colors are necessary to produce full color. For the artist, they are red, yellow and blue, but for the printer, they are *magenta* (a combination of red and blue), *cyan* (a combination of blue and green) and *yellow*. Black ink and the white of the paper stock provide the necessary values.

To reproduce full-color artwork, these three colors need to be separated. This requires the use of a filter in each of three film exposures. Red, blue, and green filters are used. These three colors are called *additive* because if mixed together, they yield white.

The process of making color negatives is complex, but is close to that used to make black and white halftone negatives. There are two basic procedures for color separating: the indirect method and the direct method. The direct method produces a screened negative as the color is separated by each filter. The indirect method first produces an unscreened positive which is color-corrected before making a screened negative. Printers prefer the indirect method because they can make color corrections by hand.

Each filter used produces a separate negative termed a *printer*. Full-color reproduction requires at least four printers: cyan, magenta, yellow, and black. (How these filters actually capture the image is too involved for our purpose; for further study, see the bibliography.) Because process colors (magenta and cyan) are not pure colors, they need to be strengthened or lessened to produce the full range of natural colors. To do this, the color separator must actually strengthen or lessen the ink. This involves a complex process called *screening*.

Note: Today, many color separations are made by completely automated scanning systems. Lasers are beamed over the artwork, and electronic devices do the color separation and color correction. Some devices use transparencies to start with; others use reflection-type work.

Where to Print in Full Color

The majority of printers are not likely to be equipped to handle full color. Others will not want to print cards even if they are capable of doing so. However, a few are both willing and able to help out. To find such printers in your area, use the telephone book. Ask for recommendations from those who do not handle cards. Most places will be more than willing to point you in the right direction.

Once you have found a printer that does print card format in full color, you will find certain options will be available. Each printer uses a limited number of paper stocks according to what type of press he owns and what type of work he normally handles. They will offer certain package deals. If you do not think a printer is offering what you are looking for, try somewhere else. *Note*: Be careful the printer is not going to send your work out to someone else to do the job.

One area where you *can* save money is in the color separation. Very few printers do their own work. They usually send out to a color separator. You can, too.

Color Separators

Color separators can be found in the yellow pages of the telephone book. By taking your artwork to them directly, you can save up to fifty percent of the separation cost. A printer will charge $300 to do the job, while a color separator will do it for $150. This cost is relative to a typical 5″ × 7″ card format. Larger jobs will cost more.

There are two ways in which you can approach a color separator with your artwork. You can bring in the actual artwork which is called *reflected art*, or you can have a large format (4″ × 5″, 8″ × 10″) positive transparency made. Color-separating from a transparency is slightly cheaper, but when the cost of the transparency is added in, the bill is just about the same. For best results, reflected art is recommended. Transparencies tend to lose some color and detail during the process.

A color separator will likely offer two methods of doing the actual work. The most common and inexpensive process involves using acetate overlays. This is referred to as a *3M* process. The other option involves *Cromalins*, or layers of thin membranes on paper. The inks are built up through the membranes which provide a solid image on paper. With 3M overlays, it is necessary to envision what the final product will look like on paper. So there is a definite advance to the Cromalin process. However, Cromalins cost approximately twenty percent more than 3M's. In the end, the card will look the same whichever process is used.

Full-Color Printing Costs

A typical card, 5″ × 7″, printed on a standard 65 lb. cover stock, should cost approximately $800 per thousand. This is for a single-fold card, and the $800 includes $300 for color separation. If you have the separation done on your own, the price would drop to $650 per thousand. This reduces the cost from $.80 to $.65 per card, which is still an overwhelming figure considering envelopes, packaging, marketing, and labor costs have yet to be included. Remember, card shops will approximately double your wholesale price. So even if your card is wholesaled for $.65, it would have to be worth $1.30 off the rack.

At this point, the situation looks forbidding, but what happens if the number printed jumps to 10,000? At 10,000, the cost could drop as low as $1600, which reflects a considerably more reasonable $.16 per card. The problem now shifts to marketing and selling 10,000 cards. There is, however, a way out of this apparent dilemma. Often, a printer is willing to print 2,000 or 5,000 cards at nearly the 10,000 rate if the artist is having several designs printed up simultaneously. This helps both parties out. As a card producer, you should try to offer as many cards as possible in your portfolio. The more you can show, the more seriously your portfolio will be taken. Showing less than twelve designs is not a solid approach, though no fixed number can be ruled out.

The bottom line is still cost-related. Whether printing 1,000 or 10,000 cards or printing two designs or twenty designs, the price remains high.

Note: The prices reflected in this chapter, high as they seem, will likely keep rising each year. This should be considered in your evaluation. It is natural to ask how even large card publishers can afford to stay in business. The answer is again found in numbers. American Greetings alone produces over ten million items every working day.

Black and White Printing Costs

As with color printing, it is the initial expense of making the plate and inking the press that accounts for the bulk of black and white printing costs. Higher volume means lower overall costs, as the price of extra paper and ink is minimal.

Standard printing paper is 8½″ x 11″. If French-folded, this gives a card size of 4¼″ × 5½″, a rather small format. The single-folded size would be 5½″ × 8½″, which is somewhat large for a card. Therefore, unless the printer is set up for card production, the paper must be trimmed down to size. All printing processes, including trimming, cutting, folding, and scoring, add extra cost.

Taking a standard 8½″ × 11″ paper stock as an example, here are some general estimates. A single color ink (black or otherwise) on a standard 65 lb. stock should run approximately $50 for one hundred. This includes the plate, ink, and paper. It may include folding as well. This translates into $.50 per card. However, a run of 1,000 costs about $90 to $100 and brings the cost of each card down to $.09, a more reasonable expense.

Two-color printing (black plus another color) will cost roughly thirty-five to forty-five percent more than one-color printing, the cost for one thousand cards being perhaps $.12 to $.14 per card.

Note: These estimates are not intended to be precise indications, only relative ones. They apply only to cards with printing on one side of the paper. Printing copy on the reverse side runs an additional ten to twenty percent. In any case, prices vary widely, and only direct estimates from your printer will determine your exact expenses.

Remember, any additional processes will add further costs, especially major ones like embossing and die cutting. Using coated or heavier paper stocks will run more as well.

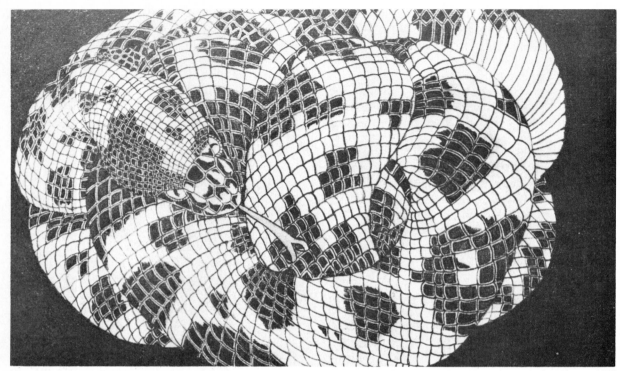

Figure 12-5
Snake design by Marion Moore. Printing in black and white is considerably less expensive than printing in full color. As a result, it is often the only option available. Courtesy of the artist, Brookline, Mass.

In the final analysis, printing a medium run of one thousand, in one or two colors is relatively inexpensive, especially when compared with the cost of printing full color. Still, if several cards are printed up at one time, the cost rises formidably. Perhaps a minimum of $1,000 should be expected to start with. If this cost appears prohibitive, there are two options: hand coloring, or printing up your own cards.

Hand-Coloring Printed Cards

The cost of having others print your cards can run high, especially where color is concerned. Black and white is cheaper to produce but harder to compete with in a market that is basically full color. One option is to have your designs printed in black and white and then add color by hand. How much color can be added depends on how large the run is and how ambitious you are. With a good system, small and medium runs of up to a thousand will probably not take as much effort as thought. Larger runs naturally take more time

and energy; but considering the alternatives, your own labor is probably the most affordable.

Note: Watercolors are great for cards that are to be photographed and printed, but are not permanent enough for hand-coloring. More permanent inks and markers are better suited for such tasks.

MAKING CARDS BY HAND

Silkscreening

Handprinting small and medium card runs can be achieved in several ways. The most prominent two methods are block printing and silkscreening. For printing in color, silkscreening is easily the most versatile process available. Figure 12-6 shows a handsome silkscreened card by Barbara Berger.

This design is one of over one hundred hand-screened cards offered in Berger's catalog. The cards are printed on a medium paper stock with

Figure 12-6
Landscape design by Barbara Berger. Silkscreening is probably the best method of hand printing cards in full color. Copyright by and courtesy of the artist.

a slight texture. The colors are flat but rich, characteristic features of the silkscreen process. Rich colors are just one of the advantages of this process; heavy, dense colors are also possible. Silkscreen inks can be applied to surfaces ranging from paper to plastic and are a favorite for printing on fabrics.

Block Prints

For black and white and limited color, block prints are a natural process. Figure 12-7 displays a linoleum block print made from the block shown in Figure 12-1. Linoleum blocks are easy to cut and quite inexpensive. The type shown in Figure 12-7 has a thin linoleum layer (1/4″) mounted on a heavier wood block. The wood provides support, as the linoleum is flexible. This block was used to make a small run of about fifty Christmas cards, but the block is still good and could produce several hundred prints if needed.

For longer runs, wood blocks will outlast linoleum blocks. They are not as popular in greeting cards partly because of the hardness of the wood. Linoleum is considerably easier to cut.

Both linoleum and wood blocks can be purchased in a variety of small sizes from your local art supply store. With a few cutting tools, blocking ink and a wood spoon (for transferring the ink onto the paper), block prints can be made. The total cost is very low. Block prints can be transferred onto a variety of paper surfaces from rice paper to heavier cover stocks.

Note: As with all printing processes, more refined, detailed prints require using smooth types of papers. A heavily textured paper will lose much in translation from the original to the paper.

Hand Stamping

Handmade stamps provide another alternative method of making a limited number of cards. Figure 12-8, by Linda Levine, shows a stamped design. This card exhibits some of the typical aspects of hand stamping. The colors show a

Figure 12-7
By Ron Lister. Linoleum block (reversed) used for Christmas linocut (Figure 12-1).

Figure 12-8
A hand stamped card by Linda Levine. Copyright by and courtesy of the artist, Cambridge, Mass.

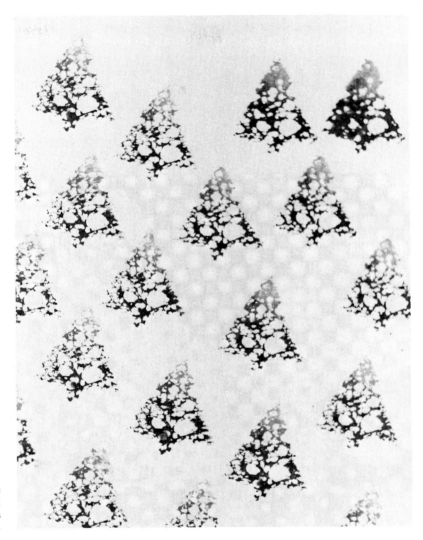

Figure 12-9
By Ron Lister. For this hand-stamped
Christmas design, a dried sponge was
cut with an exacto knife.

degree of delicate modulation, while the outline of each reindeer is markedly bold.

Hand stamps can be cut from sponges, or small pieces of rubber or linoleum, and a variety of common fruits and vegetables. Potatoes are a favorite with kids. The most permanent stamps are those cut from wood.

Note: Pre-made rubber stamps are now being sold in a variety of places.

Stenciling

Making hand stencils used to be a very popular method of making cards. Stenciling is similar to silkscreening in that certain areas are blocked out from receiving ink, or, in this case, gouache, marker, or watercolor. Stenciling is still used in lettering and sign-making. Colors can be brushed on, sprayed on, or dabbed on with a sponge. They can also be overlaid to produce deep, rich tones on a variety of different surfaces.

Papers

Artists having their cards printed up at a printer will not need to buy their own paper stock. This section is, therefore, aimed primarily at designers who are printing their own cards. My first recommendation is to stay clear of art supply stores selling small supplies of paper. The papers may be nice, but the prices are usually steep. If you need stock to print on, do some footwork. Use the Yellow Pages. Find the largest retail paper centers in your area. Wholesale paper outlets

Figure 12-10
Peace by Helen Eddy Estes. Estes' cards are printed on a
smooth, medium weight paper stock. Copyright by and
courtesy of the artist.

are for big customers only. A good retail paper
center should offer enough choices to fill your
needs.

When buying paper stock, there are two major concerns: matching the right paper to the
printing medium, and getting strong paper that
will resist rack and distribution damage. If you
are silkscreening or block printing, almost any
type of stock will do, but remember detailed,
fine-line artwork calls for smoother paper stocks
like Vellum. Other types of coated stocks, sometimes called chrome-coated or cast-coated, have

smooth surfaces as well. So, if your linoleum cut
relies heavily on fine-line work, go with a smooth
stock.

The most important concern is the paper's
strength. Buying a heavy enough stock will usually insure a good printing quality as well.

Paper Weights

Paper is sold by points or weight in pounds.
Pounds refers to how much paper weighs in a
ream. A ream is 472, 480, or 500 sheets. What
we generally need to insure a single-folded card
against damage is a minimum weight of 65 lbs.
This is equal to 8 points. Paper this strong is
divided into several name groups: cover stock,
index, or bristol. You may see vellum bristol,
quality cover, or white index. There are countless individual names given to the papers. In any
case, a 65 lb. index weight is comparable to a
standard business card or file card. A standard
manila folder is equal to an 11 pt. weight. If the
stock is 110 lb. weight, then it is that much
stronger. Cover stocks are sold normally by the
thousand, though smaller quantities can be pur-
chased. A quality vellum cover stock, $8\frac{1}{2}'' \times 11''$,
should run approximately $30 (for 1,000 with
250 sheets in each package).

When buying paper, keep in mind the weight,
texture, and, of course, the cost. Finally, if you
are going to French-fold your designs, it is possible to go with slightly lighter weight papers.

Retail Envelopes

Standard sizes of envelopes can be found wherever paper is retailed. One nice touch is to match
colored stocks with colored envelopes. Prices for
envelopes vary widely, but should cost roughly
half as much as a good sheet of cover stock.

Handmade Papers

Handmade papers are fun to work on and beautiful to look at. However, they are generally too
weak for commercial use. They are recommended only as a surface to work on, not as a
surface stock for printed cards. Handmade papers are also quite expensive, especially when
buying in quantity.

Chapter Thirteen

Selling Your Own Cards

Figure 13-1 *Zebras* by Barbara Berger. Copyright by and courtesy of Barbara Berger, Cambridge, Mass.

Handling the legal and technical aspects of a card business is a large undertaking. To do it well involves some serious thought. This chapter addresses problems that are basic to selling your own products: how to protect yourself, how to get the best tax breaks, and how to best promote and sell your cards. Many of the tips found in this section could not be classified separately, so it is suggested you read through the chapter thoroughly.

SETTING UP A BUSINESS WITHIN YOUR STATE

Legally setting up a business involves several steps. Each state has set up guidelines to go by. Unfortunately, there is no standard national guideline. Therefore, it is necessary to contact your local state government for any information they have on starting a business or incorporating a business. The telephone book will list a corporation information line and a forms supply line for receiving the correct state tax forms. You will need to get from your state an estimated tax form for the year. The letters *ES* pertain to this form, like the federal estimated tax form 1040ES.

Your state may or may not have a booklet on tax guidelines and general information. If the corporation information line cannot help, then I suggest calling the office of the secretary of state. They will know what is available.

Federal Guidelines

It is necessary to file an estimated tax form, the 1040ES, with the federal government. To get one, call your local IRS forms-only line. In smaller cities or rural areas, call your IRS information line. These estimated vouches must be filed quarterly. The government also publishes a "Tax Guide for Small Businesses." It is called Publication 334, and is printed yearly. To get one, call as early in the year as possible. Supplies often run out.

The Need for Accountants and Bookkeepers

Simply stated, a good accountant and/or bookkeeper can save you a great deal of time and money. Running a business is hard enough without having to do all the paperwork as well. Whether you need help will become apparent as your business grows.

When I first set up my own business, I sent for and received every publication on taxes available. The amount of information was overwhelming. After reading through as much as possible, I ran to locate an accountant to find out what I had read.

Basics of the Tax Game

There are literally hundreds of ways to save on taxes. As a freelance artist or small business operating out of your own residence, there are several things to know. First, in some towns, you may be required to register your intent to use part of your residence as a studio or business. A small fee may also be required. After that, it is

clear sailing. If your dwelling has five rooms and you can prove one room is used for business purposes only, you can deduct twenty percent of all bills affecting your residence. This includes heat, electricity, telephone, maintenance, and rent. Likewise, if you use a car for business purposes, gas, mileage, and maintenance can also be deducted. The list goes on; business lunches and dinners, business supplies, and anything else pertaining to the studio can be deducted from your taxes. Here is where a good accountant can help. He or she can make you aware of all the various deductions allowed by law and how to best document yourself to qualify for them at the end of the year. You will discover the many advantages of saving old receipts and using credit cards.

Copyright and Reselling Laws

Greeting cards, stationery, and paper products have held a special position in copyrighting since 1978. The law states that after 1978, artists may resell their work if no written contract has been signed between parties *and* the artist is not engaged in full-time employment by the first party. This especially affects freelance artists who have no binding contract with a publisher, though reselling one's work should always be considered thoroughly. According to the law, artists who work full-time for a company do not own the rights to their cards even if no written contract has been signed. It is understood the company owns those rights.

This law also allows artists the option of not including a copyright date along with registering. (This pertains only to pictorial graphics, not text.) The option of not including a copyright date on a design is aimed at helping artists protect themselves from outdating their designs. Even a few years after a date has been placed on a design, the card already appears old.

Copyright Registration

There are two ways to protect your work with a copyright. The first method is called *Copyright Notice* and simply involves placing your name and the copyright symbol, ©, or the word *copyright* on your card, normally on the back. A date may be included if you wish. These two

Figure 13-2
A fish design by Pat Overmoyer. Greeting cards have held a special position in copyrighting since 1978. Copyright by and courtesy of the Patsy Co.

things (name and copyright symbol) give partial protection, but only *Copyright Registration* gives you full protection. To do this, each design or related sets of designs must be registered at the Copyright Office of the Library of Congress (10 First Street, S.E., Washington, D.C. 20540). Forms are available by calling your Federal Information Center. Each city has such a center, and their number is helpful for answering any questions you may have about who and where to contact.

By registering, you are protected to the fullest by law. The fee is $10 per copyright, which is stiff if you plan to insure individual designs. This coverage is worthwhile, however, if you ever need to go to court.

Note: Copyright notice without registration only protects your artwork from being stolen. An in-court settlement for money is not likely without copyright registration. However, you should be able to stop someone else from continuing to market your design, and you may also be able to force a recall of their product. Of course, all cases are decided upon individually.

Foundations

Many states have an Arts Foundation through which legal and technical aid can be obtained. In Massachusetts, we have the Arts and Humanities Foundation, Inc. One of their functions is to periodically publish a free brochure called

Figure 13-3
Helen Eddy Estes is the co-founder of the Card Designers Network, a group located in the Boston/Cambridge area. Copyright by and courtesy of the artist.

"t.c.b." (taking care of business). It is a list of public service programs, workshops, published information, and individual counseling and professional referrals. Check your local listing. Take advantage of what is available to you through your tax dollars.

Private Groups

Sometimes, it is helpful to pool your resources together. In Boston, there is a Card Designers Network, started by a few individuals who were marketing their own cards separately. They formed a group in order to share information and reduce certain expenses. They have explored many ways of cutting down the problems that individuals face and have succeeded in some areas. This particular group has also grown considerably. You may be surprised at how many people in your area are willing to pool their resources in what is generally thought to be such a competitive field. If such a group does not exist in your area, why not start one? It is a good way to support each other while learning.

MARKETING YOUR CARDS

Making Yourself Known

It is important to remember that selling your cards depends upon making them available to the public. Doing that requires much more than simply placing them in stores. This is a business where names and reputations count. Your company, however small, must compete in a very large market, and without a name, it is difficult to be recognized. You can use your own name at first, but I recommend thinking about a trade name from the start. Design a logo. Print up business cards and self-promotional flyers and take out advertisements in trade magazines. Eventually, it is helpful to have a catalog and professional purchase orders. Start thinking about such things now. Everything associated with your business should be done professionally. If possible, have your logo and name and business address printed directly on the back of each card, rather than using a hand stamp.

Note: Some artists believe wrapping their designs in clear plastic gives them a more professional look. While the plastic does give a little added protection, it does not allow people to feel the cards and to open them up. Direct handling definitely seems to help sales, so plastic wraps are not recommended.

Selling Directly to Retail Outlets

Early on, it is likely you will be selling your cards directly to business outlets. For this, you will need a tax-exempt number called a "use and sales tax number." This gives tax exemptions to those businesses buying from you. They will have to pay a sales tax later when the card is retailed, so they will not want to pay one to you as well. To receive a tax-exempt number, contact the IRS. There is a small, one-time fee, presently $10.00.

Making direct contact with business outlets is time-consuming and fatiguing, but not really difficult. You can call individual shops for appointments, but going in person will get you further. When you are there in person, it is difficult for the buyer to refuse to look at your samples. The best approach is the direct approach. When in a shop, ask to meet the greeting card buyer. Remember, retailers are always looking for new designs, so you may be received with more interest than expected.

The most frequent concern at this point is how many samples are necessary. There is no precise answer to this, but the general rule is to show as many cards as possible. More is better. Card buyers may be reluctant to open a new account if it is small, partly because of the paperwork involved and partly because they are usually interested in long-term accounts. A small portfolio does not instill confidence either. Theoretically, you can sell one design to a buyer, but having a dozen or even two dozen samples will certainly make a big difference.

Note: Chain stores have buyers who act as distributors. These buyers purchase in larger quantities and distribute the cards to the chains. For a card producer, this is a good outlet. It means less footwork and more sales. One method of locating chain buyers is the annual buyers' list published each spring in *Greetings Magazine*. This is a voluntary list, so it is not complete. Still, it can be most helpful.

Store buyers and card producers do not like to work on consignment. Consignment is bothersome to the buyer and can be harmful to the seller. It requires extra paperwork and extra visits. Even worse, you may get back damaged cards which will never sell.

Direct sales is the standard. Small shops may exchange money upon purchase, but most likely payment will be delayed. Be sure to have a payment schedule written into your purchase order form to protect yourself. Make certain each order form is signed, and always keep the top or white copy for your records. The top copy is the legal copy.

One standard business method is termed *net* 30. It provides payment from a store within 30 days of the agreement. Some artists use discount incentives to speed up payment, but many people have complained that stores will take the discount and fail to pay in advance anyway.

In transacting business, it is helpful to have a catalog and/or order forms printed up. With printed forms, new orders can be placed over the phone, which helps the store buyers to replace your cards. Figure 13-4 shows the cover page of Daystar cards—a catalog of Helen Eddy Estes. Estes had three thousand of these two-

Figure 13-4
A *Daystar* * *catalog cover* by Helen Eddy Estes. Copyright by and courtesy of the artist.

page catalogs printed up at nearly $.50 apiece. Also included are insert order forms which add another $.05 to the total cost. This is an expensive catalog, but it looks professional. It is both attractive and functional and reflects the serious attitude of the artist.

In the beginning, it will be necessary to make return visits to stores. However, as your company grows, this will become more of a burden. In business, time is money. One way to lighten the load is through sales reps.

Sales Representatives

Sales representatives (reps) can be very helpful. Some work on their own, while others, termed sub-reps, work for larger organizations. Sales reps often work on a large scale and may not be willing to handle individual accounts. It is not easy finding good ones who are willing and able. Still, it is worth the effort. A good rep can be out

Figure 13-5
Detail of a Z fold, die cut card by Ted Naos. Copyright by and courtesy of the artist.

there selling while you are free to design new cards. In this way, your business can expand on two fronts. The sales rep will have more cards to display and will be able to reach out to new and larger buyers—buyers that could not be reached on your own. The overall idea is to be able to market *all* the cards you produce. If you can produce enough, you may end up having sales reps all over the country. There is no ideal number of reps. Start with one or two, and see how things progress.

Finding Reps

One method of locating sales reps is to ask store buyers and other artists for their names. Some people will be reluctant to help; others will not. Another method is to take out classified ads in the trade magazines. There is always a page or two of this sort in *Greetings Magazine*. Along with this, try to promote and show your work wherever you can: at crafts fairs and trade fairs, as well as with direct advertising. Once reps see your work, they may decide to come to you. This is fairly common. In fact, reps will often help promote your art through their own grapevine by telling other reps outside their own sales area about you.

Renting out a booth at the larger trade shows can be expensive, but very good for exposure. The largest and most important show, The National Stationery Show, is held each May in New York. The show attracts over seven hundred exhibitors and fourteen thousand buyers. It is currently produced by George Little Management, Inc. (Dept. GM, 261 Madison Avenue, New York, New York 10016). Be aware, however, that waiting lists for booths may be one or two years.

Also of note is a booklet titled "Beginners' Guide to New Product Publicity" by Dorothy Doty (D.D. Enterprises, P.O. Box 31, Lenox Hills Station, New York, New York 10021). The cost of the booklet is $14.95.

Profile:
Barbara Berger
on Producing Your Own Cards

Barbara Berger has been designing, printing, and marketing her own cards for the past several years. Her current catalog offers over 120 designs. The cards are silkscreened by hand (see Figures 12-6 and 13-1)

Figure 13-6
Orange Lilies by Barbara Berger. Courtesy of the artist.

and are basically floral or animal subjects. I began my interview by asking Barbara how she prepared for this career.

Barbara. I started working in art professionally late in life. I did other things and had various jobs in other fields. I always hoped I would be able to do my artwork in my spare time, which I never did. At the age of twenty-seven, I said, "Well, I'm on the wrong track, and I've got to get off fast." So I quit my job and took a few art courses on a part-time basis.

Ron. How did your business actually begin?

Barbara. My card business is an outgrowth of a project of making Christmas and Hanukkah cards for friends and family. I printed up extra cards to use as samples. I sort of got into the business as an experiment. I took samples around in January to see if I would get any orders and I did.

Ron. Where did you take them?

Barbara. I took them around to local stores, and

I got small orders but lots of encouragement. But the fact that I got any orders was encouraging to me. The shopkeepers gave me pointers, and it started up from that.

Ron. In the beginning, how did you market your cards?

Barbara. In the first year and a half, basically all I did was to make new designs because the store owners had told me I needed more designs. I started off with only eleven cards. They always like to see new things. The more cards you have to show the better. That first year and a half, I did all my own marketing.

Ron. After this time, how did you go about marketing your cards beyond your own limitations?

Barbara. It's hard to remember. I think I did approach somebody (a sales representative), and I still didn't have that many designs in my line, and they weren't interested. A shopkeeper gave me that name. Then somebody approached me; he was a new rep who had seen my cards in the shops. He was looking for lines to build up his business. Unfortunately, he didn't turn out to be as successful as I would have liked. After that, I was more assertive about getting sales reps. I put an ad in *Greetings Magazine*, and I got my best rep from that. Also, I've gotten sales reps from word of mouth. Nowadays when I inquire into the services of a rep, I always ask that if my line doesn't fit in with the other product you carry, could you please recommend me to somebody else in your territory. People have been very good about that.

Last year, I participated in the National Stationery Show in New York, and that was another good way of getting sales reps.

Ron. What is happening now?

Barbara. Last year I got a couple of good reps; previous to that, I was doing all of my own selling, and I could control my volume. But things are becoming difficult. I'm really at a crux now in my business. The only way to make money in the business is to do the biggest volume that you can possibly do and the only way I can do that volume is to stop producing my own cards and have them printed by a commercial printer.

Ron. Do you have anybody helping out?

Barbara. Yes, I contract some work to a few people, folding and such. I still do the book work myself.

Ron. Can you give one or two tips to anyone starting their own business?

Barbara. I would say do a lot of business planning first. *Do not* start out by printing your own cards. Talk to people who have their own businesses. Find out all the different things that are involved. These other things become a substantial part of your time. Learn to make a business plan first. If you don't know how, find out.

———————————————————————

Chapter Fourteen

Conclusion

a man's pool is his castle...

Figure 14-1 *A man's pool is his castle* by Daniel Katz. Copyright by and courtesy of the artist.

This book has presented many perspectives on the card and paper product field, both good and bad. For although this business can be fun and profitable, it can also be harrowing. In a way, we are constantly putting ourselves, through our art, on the line. All artistic endeavors are related in this manner. To some, this is a form of pressure. To others, it is just another chance to ex-press oneself. As much as I like painting cards and paper graphics, there are others, who for a variety of reasons, find it difficult or unsatisfying. My best advice to those who are contemplating a career in this field is not to sit on the fence wondering which way to jump. If you want to try something, do it. Do not wait. If you do jump into an area where you do not belong, then

Figure 14-2
Ten minutes of joy and laughter . . . my portfolio by John Mahoney. John Mahoney is a former card designer. He is now a working and teaching cartoonist. Courtesy of the artist, Boston, Mass.

at least you will have found out and can make the necessary adjustments. Sitting on the fence achieves nothing.

MOVING ON

A certain number of greeting card artists, no matter how successful they become, find themselves moving on to other careers. For some, designing paper products simply does not appease their artistic hunger. Others find that a card background has only led them into new areas, new fields. Anatoly Dverin is one artist who falls into both of these categories. Dverin was a very successful artist in Russia before immigrating to America in the mid-1970s. We worked closely together at Rust Craft for three years before going our own ways.

Dverin is presently a well-known book and magazine illustrator. He has always been intensely motivated to both prove himself and express his feelings. Designing paper products did not fulfill his needs in these areas but did serve as a good transitional job from one field to another. Even if designing greeting cards eventually leads to other things, it can be an important and often necessary step in the process.

Profile:
Anatoly Dverin,
Former Card Designer

Ron. As a greeting card artist, you were very successful. Why did you leave the greeting card field?

Anatoly. Because it wasn't what I wanted. I didn't like the subjects given to me, like cats, dogs. . . . I didn't like cutes.

Ron. Did they tell you too many things to do?

Anatoly. Yes, too many things, step by step, and you do what they want, not what you want. You cannot express yourself in greeting cards.

Ron. As an illustrator, you are still a freelance artist. How similar is that to your old career as a card freelancer?

Anatoly. It's very similar in certain ways. You don't know what will happen tomorrow. You have deadlines.

Ron. Do you work with the same media?

Anatoly. No, as an illustrator, I work with many media. In greeting cards, it's very limited, only gouache and watercolor. Now, I work with pastel, pen and ink, charcoal, oils. . . . You never see greeting cards in oils.

Ron. You do portraits now, too. Is that right?

Anatoly. Yes. I do portraits for magazines and on commissions. I like it.

Ron. There are no portraits in greeting cards, are there?

Anatoly. No, just once; I did Martin Luther King.

Ron. How did you establish yourself as an illustrator?

Anatoly. This was real hard. I left Rust Craft and worked for a couple of weeks at an agency. I didn't like it, so I quit and was without a job. Then I had to establish myself. I started to prepare my portfolio. For some time, I had no income. Afterwards, I made many appointments. They looked and said, "That's okay, but right now we don't have any work; we'll call you later." I thought that was baloney, but they started to call me, and after that it snowballed. Now, they say, "Recently I saw your work. . . ." Now I'm so busy, I can't find time to relax.

Ron. How long did it take to establish yourself?

Figure 14-3
Samavar by Anatoly Dverin, an
oil painting used as a calendar
design. Used by permission of
Norcross-Rust Craft Divisions of
Windsor Communications
Group, Inc.

Anatoly. I haven't peaked yet. It's always different markets. You can be busy with local markets. I'm trying to move into the national market because you will never be successful in only your local area.

Ron. Do you have any advice for people who want to get out of the card field and into another field, whatever it is?

Anatoly. You really should know what you want to do, because the competition is tremendous. It's unbelievable. If you want to do fashion, then make a straight fashion portfolio. Don't try to do too many areas. You won't be successful. Art directors have enough artists to choose from. If they need pen and ink with points (dots), they will not think that Anatoly can do some points. They will call an artist who does *only* points. So you must concentrate and be terrific in one area.

THE FUTURE

Back in Chapter One, I stated the future depends on the cards we are about to produce, that we are the deciding factor in determining what's new on the market. The greatest difference between those who will create the future and those who will not involves doing the work. Doing is what separates success from failure.

Thinking up new ideas for marketing is not really all that difficult. It is carrying through and producing those ideas in real terms that stops many of us. As we look around for the latest concepts in cards, we see imagination *and* initiative. Musical Christmas and birthday cards are now being produced; they use small computer chips triggered to sound when the card is opened.

Figure 14-4
Turkish tile. Designs for cards can come from many sources. Here a 16th century Turkish tile has been reproduced by the Isabella Stewart Gardner Museum. Courtesy of the Isabella Stewart Gardner Museum.

Figure 14-5
Have anise day by Marilyn Alexander. Copyright by and courtesy of Flavor it Cards, Whidbey Island, Wash.

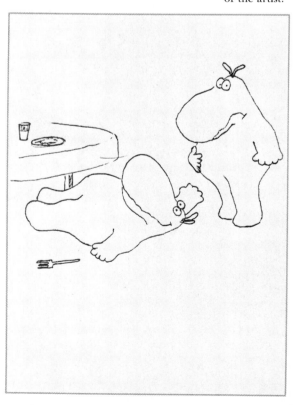

Figure 14-6
By Robert Jantzen. This is a cartoon illustrating Soft Touch Cheesecake from a proposed cookbook. Courtesy of the artist.

Figure 14-7
It's not the same here without you by Kate Whittaker. Copyright by and courtesy of Renaissance Greeting Cards, Springvale, Maine.

However, this is one of the more technically-oriented concepts in recent years. Most new ideas are not technically beyond our means. One example is the Flavor It Card series, copyrighted by Marilyn Alexander. In Figure 14-5, Alexander has cleverly packaged a standard, single-fold card to include a small sample of anise seeds.

The caption reads "Have anise day . . ." and on the back states, "In early Rome, anise flavored a favorite cake eaten after feasts to prevent tummy-ache." The entire concept is simply stated and produced. The series is displayed on its own rack in health food stores and card shops. The Flavor It Card series is a good example of a sound idea being brought to life with initiative and work.

Through the years, I have met quite a few artists whose talents fall heavily on the creative end of the scale. I have seen everything from humorous cookbooks to animated match boxes, and I have heard of countless ideas yet to be visualized. One I particularly like is post-nuclear war change-of-address cards.

For every design concept that succeeds, there are some that fail. You need to be somewhat of a gambler to produce your own ideas. Even freelancing requires some of the same instincts to survive, but one thing is certain: nobody ever succeeded who did not first try.

AND FINALLY

The card and paper fields offer a wide range of opportunities to the artist. But because the field is so large, it has become necessary to specialize. Today more than ever, it is difficult to succeed in more than one area or endeavor. Competition is strong in every area. Still, with respect for that competition and with hard work, there is room to mature and develop and room to succeed—at many different levels.

The following list of greeting card companies includes some of the larger and most consistent freelance buyers in the market. Those specializing in paper products have been noted. This listing does not contain the names of art directors because of the frequent turnover in that area. When contacting a company, you may wish to write "Attention—Art Director" on the outside of the envelope. This should suffice. Remember, when making inquiries, to include a self-addressed, stamped envelope.

ACARD Company
P.O. Box 417, South Laguna, California 92677

American Greetings Corp.
10500 American Rd., Cleveland, Ohio 44102

Antioch Publishing Co.
Box 28, Yellow Springs, Ohio 45387

Barton-Cotton Inc.
1405 Parker Rd., Baltimore, Maryland 21227

Beach Products
2001 Fulford St., Kalamazoo, Michigan 49001
(paper goods)

Carolyn Bean Publishing Ltd.
120 Second St., San Francisco, California 94105

Sidney J. Burgoyne & Sons Inc.
2120 W. Allegheny Ave., Philadelphia, Pennsylvania 19132

Cape Shore Paper Products Inc.
57 High St., South Portland, Maine 04106

H. George Caspari, Inc.
225 Fifth Ave., New York, New York 10010

CPS Industries
Columbia Hwy., Franklin, Tennessee 37064
(gift wrap only)

C.R. Gibson Company
Knight St., Norwalk, Connecticut 06856
(stationery)

Crockett Collections
Box 1428, Rt. 7, Manchester Center, Vermont 05255

The Drawing Board Greeting Cards, Inc.
8200 Carpenter Freeway, Dallas, Texas 75247

The Evergreen Press, Inc.
2479 Estand Way, Pleasant Hill, California 94523

Fran Mar Greeting Cards Ltd.
Box 1057, Mt. Vernon, New York 10550
(paper products)

Fravessi-Lamont Inc.
11 Edison Pl., Springfield, New Jersey 07081

Fremarque Publishing
Box 4577, Boulder, Colorado 30301

Grand Rapids Calendar Co.
906 S. Division Ave., Grand Rapids, Michigan 49507

Green Tiger Press
7458 La Jolla Blvd., La Jolla, California 92037

Hallmark Cards Inc.
2501 McGee, Kansas City, Missouri 64108
(does not normally buy freelance work)

Kersten Bros.
9312 N. Ninety-fourth St., Scottsdale, Arizona 85258

Laff Masters Studios Inc.
Box T, Merrick, New York 11566

Alfred Mainzer Inc.
27-08 Fortieth Ave., Long Island City, New York 11101

Mark I Inc.
1733-55 W. Irving Park Rd., Chicago, Illinois 60613

Millen Cards Inc.
45 Ranick Dr. E., Amityville, New York 11701

Museum Card Co.
Rt. 2, Clear Lake, Minnesota 55319

Pakwell Paper Products
Box 800, Wilsonville, Oregon 97070

Paper Moon Graphics
Box 34672, Los Angeles, California 90034

The Paramount Line Inc.
400 Pine St., Pawtucket, Rhode Island 02863

Peck Inc.
3963 Vernal Pike, Box 1148, Bloomington, Indiana 47402 (Christmas products)

Portal Publications Ltd.
    21 Tamal Blvd., Corte Madera, California 94925

Recycled Paper Products Inc.
    3636 N. Broadway, Chicago, Illinois 60613

Red Farm Studios
    334 Pleasant St., Pawtucket, Rhode Island 02862
    (buys little freelancing)

Renaissance Greeting Cards, Box 126, Springville,
    Maine 04083

Reproducta Co. Inc.
    11 E. Twenty-sixth St., New York, New York 10010

Rousana Cards
    28 Sager Place, Hillside, New Jersey 07205

St. Clair Pakwell
    120 Twenty-fifth Ave., Bellwood, Illinois 60104
    (packaging and gift wraps)

Sunrise Publications Inc.
    Box 2699, Bloomington, Indiana 47402

Tuttle Press Co.
    Box 759, Appleton, Wisconsin 54912
    (paper products)

Westvaco, C.A. Reed Division
    99 Chestnut St., Williamsport, Pennsylvania 17701
    (paper products)

Williamhouse-Regency Inc. & Century Greetings
    1500 W. Monroe St., Chicago, Illinois 60607
    (Christmas cards)

Bibliography

Card-Related Subjects

Berlye, Milton K., *How to Sell Your Art Work*. Englewood Cliffs, N.J.: Prentice-Hall, Inc., 1978.

Chase, Ernest D. *The Romance of Greeting Cards*. Cambridge, Mass.: University Press, 1958.

Davis, Sally A. *1982 Artist's Market*. Cincinnati, Ohio: Writers Digest Books, published yearly.

Gray, Bill. *Studio Tips*. New York, N.Y.: Von Nostrand Reinhold Co.
———. *More Studio Tips*. New York, N.Y.: Van Nostrand Reinhold Co.

Itten, Johannes. *The Art of Color*. New York, N.Y.: Van Nostrand Reinhold Co., 1973.

Muse, Ken. *The Secrets of Professional Cartooning*. Englewood Cliffs, N.J.: Prentice-Hall, Inc., 1981.

Printing

Prust, Z.A. *Photo-Offset Lithography*. South Holland, Ill.: Goodheart-Willcox Co. Inc., 1977.

Stone, Bernard, and Arthur Eckstein. *Preparing Art for Printing*. New York, N.Y.: Van Nostrand Reinhold Co., 1965.

Termini, Maria. *Silkscreening*. Englewood Cliffs, N.J.: Prentice-Hall, Inc., 1978.

General Books

Derkatch, Inessa. *Transparent Watercolor*. Englewood Cliffs, N.J.: Prentice-Hall, Inc., 1980.

Edwards, Betty. *Drawing from the Right Side of the Brain*. Los Angeles, Calif.: J.P. Tarcher, Inc., 1979.

Hiller, J. *Utamaro*. New York, N.Y.: E.P. Dutton, 1979.

Lister, Ron. *Drawing with Pastels*. Englewood Cliffs, N.J.: Prentice-Hall, Inc., 1981.

Index